THE MAPMAKERS

A HISTORY OF STANFORDS

This edition published by Compendium
43 Frith Street, London, W1D 4SA, UK

A CIP Catalogue record for this book is available
from the British Library

1-902579-75-5

Printed in Hong Kong through Printworks Int. Ltd.

*This publication has been generously supported
by Anne Vallings, who is from a distinguished map
family*

THE MAPMAKERS

A HISTORY OF STANFORDS

Peter Whitfield

Foreword by Nicholas Crane

Three hundred years before the Stanford story opened in Charing Cross, a London printer called John Daye pulled from his press a new translation of Euclid's *Elements of Geometry*. The Preface had been written by Elizabeth I's alchemic mathematician, John Dee. In a section of the Preface subtitled 'Geographie', Dee lost himself in a reverie upon the wondrous applications of maps and globes. They could be used to 'beautifie' halls and libraries, to locate historical events, to measure distances, to plan journeys 'into farre landes', and to follow 'other mens travailes'. By the time Dee had completed his list, almost everyone in the known universe had a reason for studying geography: 'some, for one purpose: and some, for an other, liketh loveth, getteth, and useth, Mappes, Chartes, & Geographicall Globes'.

Dee was ahead of the game. Towards the end of his life, he manipulated maps to support his scheme for a 'Brytish Impire' – an empire which would indeed spread across the unmapped Earth to create an insatiable demand for up-to-date cartography. This book describes how the dynasty reacted to that demand. It is a story which has not been told before, and it works on many levels. We learn of Victorian retailing, and the role Stanfords played in charting the last blanks on the world map. A huge, luminary cast ranges from Captain Scott to Florence Nightingale, with frequent appearances by three of the greatest institutions in map and travel publishing – John Murray, the Ordnance Survey and the Royal Geographical Society. Of overriding value is the book's insight into the rarely-documented world of commercial mapmaking.

Stanfords could not have prospered for so long without sound business timing, and their 150th anniversary occurs as mapmaking undergoes the greatest change since the introduction five hundred years ago of woodcut and copper-plate printing. Satellites and computers are enabling a generation of electronic cartographers to work with barely-imaginable accuracy and versatility. The Ordnance Survey has created the world's largest single spatial database; one, big, 'intelligent' map which records the co-ordinates of 440 million natural and manmade objects. It is updated 5,000 times a day. Virtual maps are in our cars, on laptops, on phone screens and in Stanfords.

Like thousands of others, I first came to Stanfords because I'd been told that it was the best map shop in the country. But I was unprepared for the sheer volume of geographical goodies: shelves of globes reached the ceiling and vast map chests stood islanded by cartographic strata. I'd never seen so many travel books in one place. The trip to Stanfords became a regular pilgrimage; the most enjoyable part of planning each expedition or journey. Whether I was bound for Tibet, Afghanistan, Lapland or the Norfolk Broads, I knew that I would leave with the best available maps. On one occasion, I breezed into the shop and asked for all the large-scale maps necessary to walk across Europe – a distance of 10,000 kilometres. The manager, Douglas Schatz, devoted the entire morning to accumulating a hillock of cartography ranging from Spanish military surveys to a Ukrainian road atlas. I staggered out with a bulging rucksack and spent the next day cutting the edges off the maps to save weight. Those maps endured storms, droughts, spilled sardines and months of snow. I have them now, battered and stained. They brought me home. As a traveller and inveterate map-consumer, may I take this opportunity to thank Stanfords for their unassailable services to the world of 'Mappes, Chartes, & Geographicall Globes'.

Nicholas Crane
London, 2003

Nicholas Crane is the author of *Clear Waters Rising: A Mountain Walk Across Europe*, and *Two Degrees West: An English Journey*. His most recent book *Mercator: The Man Who Mapped the Planet*, is the first English-language biography devoted to the world's greatest mapmaker. The historian Lisa Jardine described *Mercator* as a 'gripping' tale of 'heart-stopping excitement, suspense, triumph and tragedy.'

Contents

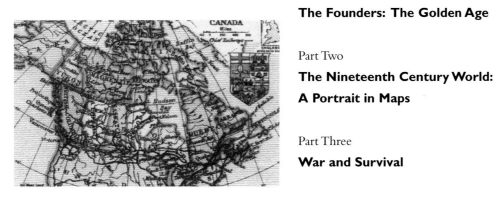

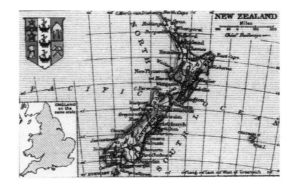

Preface

This book is a celebration of the history of Stanfords, map sellers extraordinary, now established in London's Charing Cross and Covent Garden area for one hundred and fifty years. It tells the story of how a mere shop became an institution – a fountainhead of geographical information valued by so many. The mid-nineteenth century, when Stanfords was founded, saw a tremendous increase in the use of maps by individuals and by organisations: maps became a familiar part of the social and professional landscape in a way that they had never been before. The essence of Stanford's success was to perceive this historical development, and to exploit it in various ways. For this reason, Stanford's history holds up a mirror to its age, bringing into focus many of the social and political themes of the time.

Much of this history has had to proceed by inference, because, sadly, no real company archive has survived. We know that huge quantities of documents were destroyed when the firm moved from Cockspur Street to Long Acre in 1901, and again in the 1950s, after the sale of Stanfords to George Philip. A series of business letters from the second Edward Stanford written between 1892 and 1917 is the only real source of background information that we have, and there are a thousand questions about how the maps were conceived, produced and sold which we cannot answer. Stanford left the mapmaking work in the hands of his chief cartographer, John Bolton, but of Bolton's correspondence and working papers almost nothing has survived. The one great tangible source that we have is the many hundreds of maps which Stanford published, and which offer such a rich picture of the Victorian world; therefore this book concentrates to a considerable extent on these maps, trying to place them in their historical context. For its entire history the Stanford name has been linked with that of the Ordnance Survey, but because the history of the Survey has been extensively researched and described, I have highlighted instead Stanford's role as a publisher of international maps.

Much of the detailed history of the publishing business has been impossible to recover. What Augustine Birrell wrote of the book trade is equally true of the map trade: "No great trade", he lamented, "has an obscurer history. It seems to be choked in mountains of dust, which it would be suicidal to disturb. Men have lived from time to time with literary skill who had knowledge of the traditions and practices of

'The Trade', but nobody has ever thought it worth his while to make a record of his knowledge, which perished with him, and is now irrecoverably lost." I can only hope that this book stirs a little of the dust, and may lead to further research into the fascinating world of nineteenth-century mapping.

I must thank several people who shared their expert knowledge with me while I was writing this book: Andrew Cook, Kenneth Winch, Roger Hunter, Bill Willett and Ralph Hyde. Ian and James Stanford let me into a number of family secrets concerning their respective fathers, Fraser Stanford and J.K. Stanford. Much of the research for this book was carried out at the Bodleian Library, and it is a pleasure to thank the staff there for their friendly assistance. My greatest debts are to Douglas Schatz, who commissioned and supported the project throughout, and to Francis Herbert, who knows more about the history of Stanfords than anybody else, but is too busy to write it down, and who agreed to help me instead. Many of the maps illustrated in this book are from national collections, but where no source is given, the pictures are in private hands, most of them in Stanford's company archive.

Stanfords has carried out a number of strategic shifts of direction in its long history, some by choice, some forced upon it. Its great days as a map publisher were over by the 1930s; but as a supplier of specialist world-wide mapping it has never been rivalled, and it has guarded its reputation well. In another hundred and fifty years will maps still be published and sold? Or will they have been replaced by ghastly electronic location-finders, flashing and bleeping, which we plug directly into our heads, or our car steering wheels? If so, I would be willing to bet that Stanfords will still be selling them.

RIGHT: **The Stanford heartland of Charing Cross and Long Acre, from the 1912 catalogue.**

7

Introduction

In the winter of 1887 John Ruskin, art historian, moralist and passionate critic of Victorian society, sits in Brantwood, his house above Coniston Water, brooding on the condition of England – among other things on the railways which have recently invaded the tranquillity of the Lake District. Ruskin's mind is deeply shadowed, and in these last years of his life days of lucidity would alternate with longer periods of depression and near paralysis. He has been holding informal classes for some of the local school children, trying to remedy the defects of their education, and it was in connection with these classes that he sent off a brief letter on 9 February to a London publisher:

> "Gentlemen,
> Have you any school atlas or any other sort of atlas on sale at present without railroads in its maps? Of all the entirely odd stupidities of modern education, railroads in maps are the infinitely oddest to my mind.
> Ever your faithful servant and victim
> J. Ruskin"

The surprised recipient of this strange appeal was the house of Edward Stanford, the London map seller who, in the three decades since he commenced in business, had made himself pre-eminent in his field. Stanford's fame was already immense: whether for an Ordnance Survey map of the English countryside, a map of the Balkan war-zones, of the railways of India, or of the goldfields of South Africa, Stanfords was acknowledged to be the first port of call. In *The Hound of the Baskervilles,* Conan Doyle has Sherlock Holmes "send down to Stanfords" for a large-scale map of Dartmoor, knowing that all his readers will immediately recognise the name. Stanfords had in fact established itself as one of those elite London shops, like Hatchard's, Ackermann's, Lock's, or Purdey's, which it was an experience to visit, and it was therefore inevitable that Ruskin should appeal to Stanfords and to no one else. At this time Stanfords had in fact two substantial premises in central London, one at Charing Cross and the other in Long Acre, where maps went through all their stages of production – conception, information retrieval, drawing, editing, engraving, printing, mounting, and sale to the public.

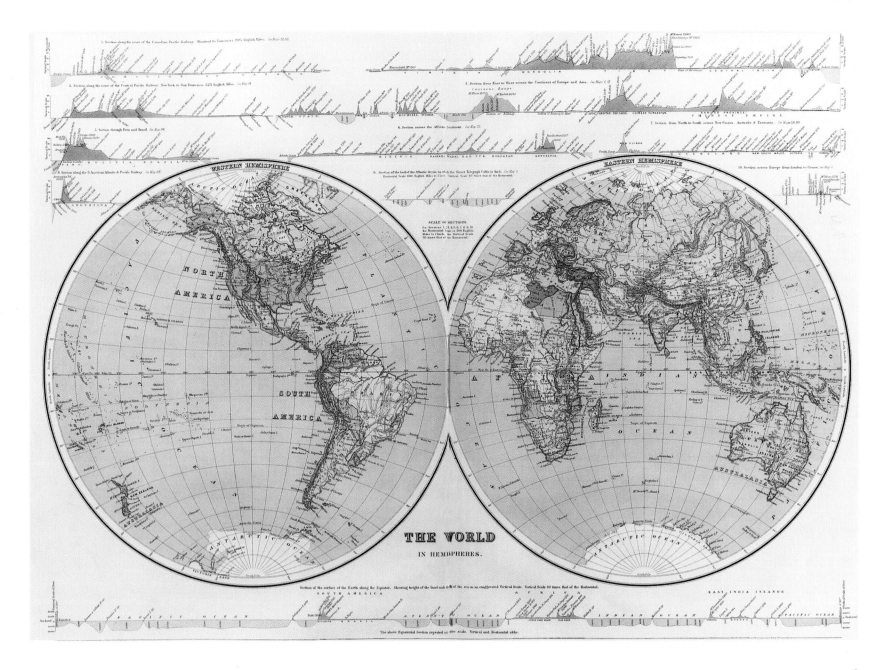

THE WORLD
IN HEMISPHERES.

The business was not huge, but it grew to employ seventy or eighty people, and it created considerable wealth for the founder's family. But the great historical interest of Stanford's map publishing activity is that it offers us a window on so many aspects of the Victorian world – commercial, political and intellectual. We may think of maps as simple, functional documents, designed to present geographical data. But this is a simplistic view, for maps are not objective pictures of reality; the truth is that into the making of maps go the aims, the beliefs, the priorities, the prejudices and the tastes of each generation. Moreover a society which is static will have little use for maps, especially for new maps, while a dynamic society will constantly make new maps to chart its changing world, and no society had been more dynamic than that of Victorian England. Map publishing thrives on change, and Ruskin was clearly in an eccentric minority, for no sensible person would accept, much less desire, a map of England which did not show the railways which now ran masterfully across the entire nation. Edward Stanford recognised that the cities and the countryside of England were changing rapidly; that the business of Empire sent thousands of travellers every year to the four corners of the world; that government administration required accurate maps to carry on its ever-expanding work, in Britain and abroad; that science was increasingly able to chart not only the surface of the earth, but its geology, its oceans, its climates, its peoples and the stars above it. He aimed to satisfy all these latent demands by supplying maps not only to the private traveller, but to the soldier, the explorer, the administrator and the scientist. Maps embodied knowledge and conferred power – this was the essence of their appeal, and of the business opportunity they presented. Stanford was not the only map publisher in Victorian England, but his range was the widest. Between 1850 and 1900 Stanford built up a rich catalogue of maps and geographical books which held up a sharply focussed mirror to the Victorian world.

The Stanford name became popularly known in connection with Ordnance Survey maps, but in this his role was that of retailer and distributor. It was above all in his role as a publisher of international maps that Stanford created a unique position. Britain was deeply involved politically and commercially with so many regions of the world: India, Southern and Western Africa, Australasia, the Middle East, the Pacific and Caribbean Islands, and South-East Asia. From virtually all these areas of the world, Stanford was able to obtain the best available survey information and produce practical, well-designed reference maps. So successful were these maps that they were bought not only by travellers to those regions, but by the government departments which administered them, and by libraries and institutions everywhere. The great offices of state – the War Office, the Foreign Office, the Commonwealth Office and the India Office – were among Stanford's regular customers, and the maps which these departments used in their work, often with important annotations, are now preserved in the Public Record Office.

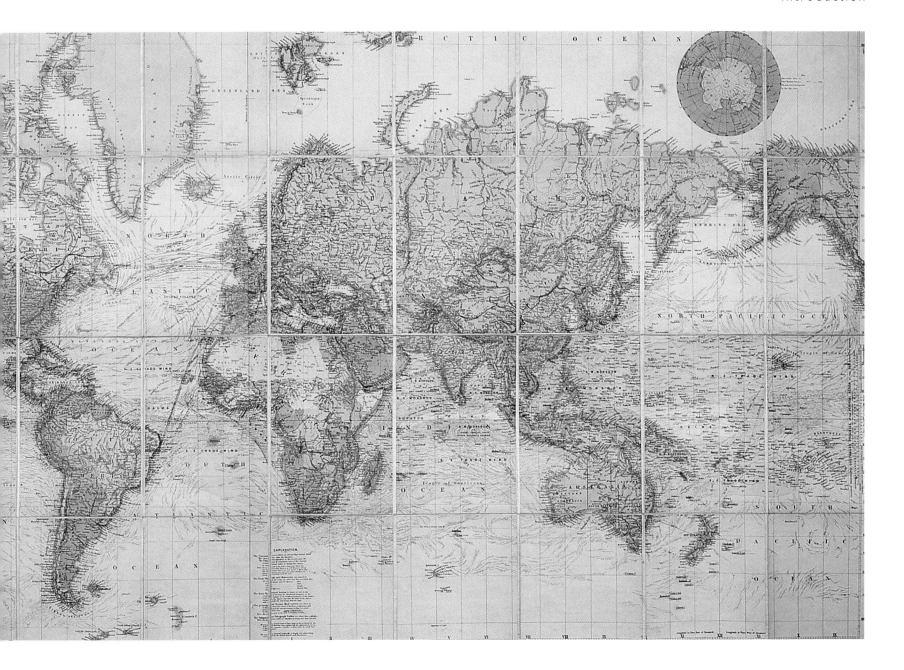

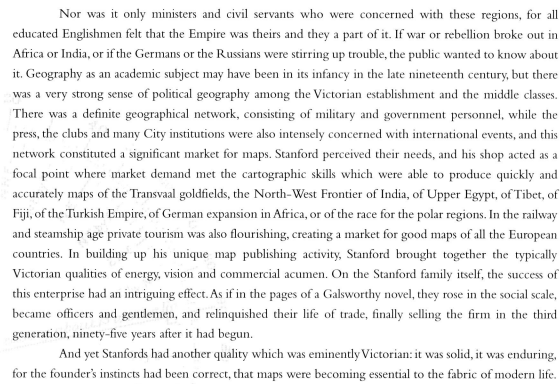

Nor was it only ministers and civil servants who were concerned with these regions, for all educated Englishmen felt that the Empire was theirs and they a part of it. If war or rebellion broke out in Africa or India, or if the Germans or the Russians were stirring up trouble, the public wanted to know about it. Geography as an academic subject may have been in its infancy in the late nineteenth century, but there was a very strong sense of political geography among the Victorian establishment and the middle classes. There was a definite geographical network, consisting of military and government personnel, while the press, the clubs and many City institutions were also intensely concerned with international events, and this network constituted a significant market for maps. Stanford perceived their needs, and his shop acted as a focal point where market demand met the cartographic skills which were able to produce quickly and accurately maps of the Transvaal goldfields, the North-West Frontier of India, of Upper Egypt, of Tibet, of Fiji, of the Turkish Empire, of German expansion in Africa, or of the race for the polar regions. In the railway and steamship age private tourism was also flourishing, creating a market for good maps of all the European countries. In building up his unique map publishing activity, Stanford brought together the typically Victorian qualities of energy, vision and commercial acumen. On the Stanford family itself, the success of this enterprise had an intriguing effect. As if in the pages of a Galsworthy novel, they rose in the social scale, became officers and gentlemen, and relinquished their life of trade, finally selling the firm in the third generation, ninety-five years after it had begun.

And yet Stanfords had another quality which was eminently Victorian: it was solid, it was enduring, for the founder's instincts had been correct, that maps were becoming essential to the fabric of modern life. Despite the severance of the family connection the business has survived and flourished down to the present day, and is still trading in Long Acre, still selling maps of an ever-changing world. In the century and a half since the business was founded, huge quantities of documents have inevitably been destroyed (we do not know, for example, what the official reply to Ruskin may have been, although he would undoubtedly have been assured that, for a price, he could have any kind of map that he wished especially drawn for him); but enough has survived to compose this brief portrait of the company, and to celebrate the unique place which it created in the history of cartography.

Part One **The Founders: The Golden Age**

The Stanford story begins not with the founder himself, the first Edward Stanford, but with another important figure in the world of nineteenth-century mapmaking, Trelawney William Saunders. Born in Plymouth in 1821, Saunders came to London at the age of eighteen to take up work with the well-known Bible publisher, Samuel Bagster. Much later Saunders would recall almost freezing to death on that youthful journey, crossing Salisbury Plain in a snowstorm on the outside of a coach. Saunders was a religious man, a member of the Plymouth Brethren, and he soon developed a special interest in the geography of the Bible, and then in maps in general. He learned the publishing trade, he prospered and married, and in 1846 he took over a stationer's shop at number 6 Charing Cross, which stood then at the northern end of

BELOW: **Charing Cross in 1869, with Stanford's first shop on the left.**

Whitehall opposite the statue of Charles I. The site is significant, for Charing Cross had been for centuries the hub of London, the place where proclamations were read and notices displayed. In the seventeenth and eighteenth centuries it was proverbial that anyone wishing to know what was happening – in London or the world – had merely to go to Charing Cross to be told. It was also the place where felons were pilloried and where the regicides had been executed at the Restoration. As a site for selling books, maps and stationery, it could hardly be bettered. All the offices of government were at hand in Whitehall, as were the gentlemen's clubs in nearby St.James's; immediately to the east, the Strand was a thoroughfare of shops and coffee-houses which led directly into the City. The shops of the leading map publishers, Thomas Jefferys and William Faden, had made Charing Cross a centre of map selling since the early eighteenth century. Here

BELOW: **Charing Cross in 1869, with Stanford's first shop on the left.**

Saunders built up his business and his special reputation for maps. In 1851 he drew a weather chart of the British Isles, and sent it, up-dated each day, to the Great Exhibition in Hyde Park. He did not publish maps himself, but he issued catalogues offering for sale a wide range of maps by English and foreign publishers.

In October 1852 Saunders accepted into partnership the young Edward Stanford, whom he had already known for some years, and within a few months, by early 1853, maps bearing the imprint Saunders and Stanford were being produced, among them maps of Africa and Australia. It seems possible that this partnership was intended from the first as a transitional arrangement, and that Saunders was planning to quit the business and steer his career into new channels. This supposition arises from the fact that in July 1853, after a mere ten months, the partnership was dissolved, and the house of Edward Stanford was born. The two men seem to have parted on good terms, for they later cooperated on many projects. Saunders subsequently wrote books on geographical subjects, and edited a number of important maps. In 1854 he became librarian and map curator first to the Royal Geographical Society and then at the India Office. He became something of an elder statesman in the world of Victorian geography, but he never achieved the outstanding success which he had aspired to. When he died in 1910 in his ninetieth year, he was blind, impoverished and forgotten, and those who learned of his passing were astonished, supposing him to have died long before. Meanwhile the business which he had handed over to Stanford had flourished and become a major force in the world of mapmaking. Who then was Edward Stanford, and how did he build so effectively on the modest beginnings made by Trelawney Saunders?

We know comparatively little about the life and personality of this man. He was born on 31 May 1827 in Holborn, the son of William and Ann Stanford, who were tailors and drapers of 29 Holborn Hill. Thus he came from that great class of urban tradesmen and shopkeepers – tailors, cabinet makers, cutlers, apothecaries, barbers, boot makers – who inhabited a Dickensian world of work, subservience and anonymity, but who would occasionally produce a genius such as Blake or Turner. As far as we know there was no connection with two other famous Stanfords: Leland Stanford, the American millionaire and founder of Stanford University; and the composer Charles Villiers Stanford. Stanford began his education at the City of London School, but at the age of fourteen he was apprenticed to a printer in Malmesbury in Wiltshire. Why he was sent to Malmesbury when he might surely have been apprenticed to any one of scores of printers in London, we do not know; it may have been because of the health problems which would later shorten his active career. At all events he did not complete his apprenticeship to become a master printer because his employer died in 1844, and Stanford returned to London at the age of seventeen, finding employment with printers and retailers of stationery, including Thomas Pettitt, the diary maker of Compton

OPPOSITE: **Stanford's shop decorated with flags for the London visit of the Czar of Russia in May 1874.**

OPPOSITE: **The first Edward Stanford
(1827–1904).
The second Edward Stanford
(1856–1917).**

Street, Soho. In 1848 he actually worked for a brief period for Trelawney Saunders, which must have formed his introduction to the world of maps. When he returned to Saunders in 1852, he presumably bought himself into the partnership, while Saunders perhaps saw Stanford's investment as his opportunity to move into a new career. It seems reasonable to see Trelawney Saunders as a crucial influence in Stanford's life, first by opening his eyes to the potential of commercial map selling, and then by offering him the chance to assume control of his own business. Saunders proposed Stanford for the fellowship of the Royal Geographical Society in 1853, thus introducing him into the select geographical fraternity of Victorian England. So Edward Stanford at the age of twenty-six found himself the sole proprietor of a small specialist shop selling books, stationery and maps. In 1855 he would marry Mary Baker, the daughter of a Harrow bookseller, and they lived together above the shop, for it was here that their son, the second Edward Stanford was born in 1856.

At the outset the shop had been simply a retail outlet, buying in goods from publishers and selling them on to the public. It may have been Stanford's experience as a printer which made him realise that greater profits were to be made if one could both produce and sell maps, just as the stationers with whom he had worked produced the diaries, calendars or account books which they sold. It seems significant that the Saunders and Stanford publishing activity began so soon after Stanford arrived. Another vital factor must have been Stanford's experience with customers in the shop: each day he was in the position of being asked for maps, whether of London, or Canada, or India or the Cape Colony, and he soon came to know which could be supplied and which could not. For an alert, intelligent businessman, the shop functioned as a superb market research facility. Why not use this knowledge to publish one's own maps? In this way he would build his reputation and his customer base: if his clients took home a Stanford map to study, they would identify his name with maps, and return to him for all future map needs. Stanford must have been aware of the other London map sellers who published their own material, such as James Wyld, G.W. Bacon and, for nautical charts, the firm of Imray, and there seems no doubt that he aspired to rival and then to outdistance them. The most striking thing about these first few years is the speed and energy with which Stanford set about building a publishing operation, and this in turn suggests that he had access to excellent funds, either from the profits of his shop, or in the form of investment capital. He seems to have envisaged from the first that the shop and the publishing activity would feed each other, creating an unrivalled centre for geographical information, and in this he was to prove absolutely correct.

There is nothing in Stanford's background to suggest that he had any special expertise in mapmaking or in geography, so from the first he employed expert cartographic draughtsmen and editors,

THE SECOND EDWARD STANFORD

Nov 13/84

10, SOUTH STREET,

PARK LANE. W.

Dear Sir

I cannot thank you enough for your great kindness in mounting the two Irrigation Maps of India so neatly & so promptly. They were quite in time. Pray believe me

yours most faithfully

Florence Nightingale

Edwd. Stanford Eq.

OPPOSITE: **Message from Florence Nightingale thanking Stanfords for a mounted map; the date is uncertain – it might be 1864 or 1884.**

while he managed the business. It was in fact impossible to study geography in any academic sense in England at this time, for it was not taught at schools or in universities. Surveying and map-drawing could be learned in the army, or from a commercial map-maker. In order to acquire quickly a world-wide map-base, Stanford bought the stock and the printing-plates of the maps which had been published in the 1830s and 40s by the S.D.U.K. – the Society for the Diffusion of Useful Knowledge, which had ceased publishing in 1846. This body had produced many excellent publications which could be marketed cheaply because its authors worked for little or no remuneration, and its many maps were among the best of their day. Stanford sold their large, two-volume atlas containing 225 maps, and he sold the maps individually for 6d plain, or 9d lightly coloured with a water-colour wash. He used a selection of twenty-nine of these maps to form *The Harrow Atlas of Modern Geography* for use in Harrow School. But Stanford had higher ambitions than merely to recycle existing maps; he wished instead to issue new, high-quality reference maps of all the regions of the world, and topical maps which would catch the public interest in special areas. To fulfil these ambitions he needed the help of a team of geographical editors, and he showed great energy in enlisting the aid of official survey authorities, army officers, geologists and hydrographers. Above all perhaps, he turned in the late 1850s to his former partner, Trelawney Saunders, to help plan and edit a series of spectacular international reference maps.

In order to appreciate the way Stanford built his business in these early years, it is necessary to understand something of the context in which he was working – the geographical scene in mid-century England – for there were a number of factors which combined to create both a strong demand for maps and a supply of the data necessary to make them. These factors included Britain's role as a colonial and maritime power; the exploration of major unmapped areas of the world; the rise of geography as an academic discipline; the work of the Ordnance Survey in producing a national map-base; and the growth of tourism to international destinations.

Through a succession of voyages of exploration, wars and treaties, Britain had come to exercise control over territories in almost every region of the world. Commercial activity, geographical exploration and land apportionment were being carried out in nearly all of these territories, creating a need for maps, while their government was conducted ultimately from London, via the Foreign Office, the Commonwealth Office and the India Office. Sustaining the colonial administration, was of course military and naval power. The need for reliable survey maps of the colonies was recognised early; in India official surveying bodies were in existence as early as the 1770s, and the Trigonometrical Survey was formally created in 1818. The surveying activity itself was carried out by trained army personnel, a pattern repeated in all British colonies. The results of these surveys were published piecemeal, in maps of the areas of special interest, as happened in the Cape Colony, the Gold Coast, Canada or New Zealand, while the Survey of India boasted a complete survey of the whole country at four miles to one inch in several hundred sheets. The Survey of India was also responsible for mapping adjacent areas such as Persia and Burma. But it was not the role of these survey authorities to publish general reference maps of their countries, and this fact presented commercial map-publishers with obvious opportunities to edit survey information into practical smaller-scale maps. Stanford was foremost in seizing these opportunities.

But Britain was also a European power, and rivalry with France, Russia and Germany was very much carried into colonial affairs, so that the European "balance of power" was the overriding concern even in India or Africa or China. British foreign policy in the nineteenth century had a number of dominant themes, the clearest example being the perennial suspicion that the Russians nursed territorial ambitions throughout Asia, and that they might ultimately threaten India itself. This fear explains the long-standing preoccupation with the countries bordering India: Persia, Tibet and Afghanistan. Lord Curzon remarked that "Frontiers are the razor's edge on which hang suspended the issue of war or peace and the life of nations." Maps were essential in following events on these frontiers, and from the outset central Asia formed a major focus of Stanford's map-publishing activities. By the mid-1870s the Intelligence Division of the War Office was active in gathering data from such border regions, and it soon initiated its own mapping programme, much of it restricted, but some of it made public via a publishing arrangement with Stanford. So expert was the Intelligence Division at feeding information back to London that one officer remarked that "the world has become a vast Anglo-Saxon whispering gallery, and that the centre of the Empire at once responds to the smallest shock experienced at any one of its extremities."

The other official form of international mapping was the sea-charts published by the British Admiralty. Formally established in 1795, the Hydrographic Office was engaged in a worldwide reconnaissance which consolidated Britain's imperial role. In some ways easier to carry out than topographic surveying because of the freedom of the seas, this charting programme had resulted in more than one thousand published charts by 1850. British hydrographic charts were sold to the public by specialised chart agents such as R.H. Laurie or John W. Norie, who also published nautical charts of their own, and by other leading map suppliers including Stanford.

The official mapping of Britain was of course in the hands of the Ordnance Survey, whose culture and senior staff were still thoroughly military in character, and whose maps were invaluable in an age of urban expansion, railway building and administrative reform. By 1860, the Ordnance Survey was engaged

LEFT AND RIGHT: **The Ruskin letter of February 1887.**

9th Feb 87
Brantwood,
Coniston. Lancashire
Messrs Stanford & Co
Gentlemen,
Have you any school atlas or any other sort of atlas on sale at present without railroads in its maps? Of all the entirely odd stupidities of modern education, railroads in maps are the infinitely oddest to my mind.

Ever your faithful
servant and victim

J. Ruskin

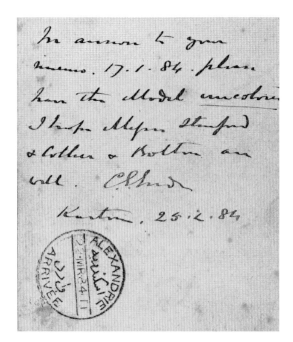

ABOVE: **Card from General Gordon, posted in Khartoum in February 1884, about some work which the firm was carrying out for him, and hoping that his friends in Stanfords were all well.**
The British Library

in a programme to map Britain at three basic scales: at one inch to one mile, at six inches to one mile, and at twenty-five inches to one mile. These maps offered the commercial map trade immense business opportunities for map sales, and they provided an unrivalled source of British topographic data for reduction to general maps. At this stage, the copyright rule was applied only to the direct copying of Ordnance maps, while the principle that all topographic data must be indebted to the Survey had not yet evolved. Stanford's dealings with the Ordnance Survey over a hundred and fifty years were to be crucial to the business of the firm, although relations between publisher and retailer were often stormy. By the mid-1870s when all these series were complete, a commercial stock of them (i.e. several copies of each sheet) would amount to almost half a million maps. At that date the Ordnance Survey's own records show that around one quarter of all their map sales were through Stanford's shop. This side of Stanford's business generated a vital source of income, but it produced, as can well be imagined, huge problems in handling, storage and customer service. To many people, Stanfords and the Ordnance Survey were indistinguishable, and the proprietor and his staff therefore received endless flak about the accuracy and availability of these huge map series.

Map publishing thrives on change – change in politics, in society and in geographical knowledge – and in the mid nineteenth century vast areas of the globe were still in the process of being explored and mapped. In the interiors of Africa, Asia and Australia, the aim of removing blanks from the map became an object of scientific and national pride. British geographical exploration had become increasingly the business of the Royal Geographical Society (R.G.S.), which had been founded in 1830. As distinct from imperial ambitions or military intelligence-gathering, the aim of the R.G.S. was to advance geographical science and to diffuse geographical knowledge. The R.G.S. sponsored many of the most important expeditions in Africa, Asia and the Polar Regions, and helped to make explorers such as Livingstone and Franklin national figures. The *Journal of the R.G.S.* established itself at once as the principal focus of geographical science and reports from around the world, and Stanford lost little time in having himself appointed official sales agent for its *Proceedings* from 1855, and later, from 1893, for *The Geographical Journal*. Side by side with exploration, the aim of the R.G.S. was to foster the teaching of geography, to raise it to the status of an academic study. This had already been achieved in Germany under the influence of Alexander von Humboldt and Carl Ritter, and there were geographical institutes in many German universities, but this movement did not reach Britain until the 1870s. The central doctrine preached by members of the R.G.S. was that when the exploration, the reconnaissance, of the entire earth's surface was complete, as it very soon would be, then a new task of scientific analysis and description must begin, which would embrace landforms, climates, peoples, wildlife and so on, and would assess how all these factors reacted with each other to produce the total environment: this was to be the new science of geography. Halford Mackinder's appointment as the first Reader in Geography at Oxford University in 1887 was a milestone in the recognition of the new subject, and the R.G.S. paid half his stipend. The spread of geographical teaching through universities and schools clearly offered new opportunities to map publishers to broaden their traditional markets.

The traditional geographical network, military and scientific, was served by a number of commercial map publishers, but Stanford seems to have set out to create the widest range of detailed, up-to-date international mapping. The other great names in this field were George Philip and John Bartholomew. Philip, a Liverpool firm which opened a London office in Fleet Street in the same year in which Stanford commenced his partnership with Saunders, chose at an early stage to concentrate on educational publications, primarily atlases, while Bartholomew did not publish under his own name until the 1890s, but carried out cartographic work for other publishers. Bartholomew moreover was an Edinburgh firm, and had no London showroom. For Stanford there was no conflict between the detailed, multi-sheet official map series issued by the Ordnance Survey, the Survey of India or the Hydrographic Office, and the general maps produced by the commercial map publisher; on the contrary the fact that they were sold together by the same firm was seen in some sense as a guarantee, making the shop a centre of geographical expertise. Stanford was quick to secure sales agencies for all these official bodies in the early 1850s, and he was anxious to announce that his own maps were based on the best official surveys. A typical wording appears on his 1856 map of the Province of Canterbury, New Zealand: "From Admiralty Charts and Colonial Surveys, with communications from colonists." An even earlier publication, a chart of the siege of Sebastopol in 1854, a crucial episode in the Crimean War, was "Compiled from the new Admiralty Charts". Then as now, war was a great stimulus to the public demand for maps.

Aside from this semi-official geographical network, what of private travel in the nineteenth century? In this field the railways had initiated a revolution, reaching across Europe from Scandinavia to the Mediterranean. The days of the leisured, wealthy traveller who must hire a series of carriages for a month's journey from a Channel port to Italy were gone, while the steamship brought Egypt and the Holy Land within easy reach. Even within Europe the tourist's horizon was now almost limitless: the Norwegian Fjords, the Swiss Alps, the antiquities of Greece, all were now accessible. This was the age of Murray's *Handbooks,* and their imitators, the Baedeker *Guides,* full of advice for the civilised traveller on the art, traditions, archaeology, scenery, railways and hotels of Europe. The 1850s also saw the first of Thomas Cook's tours to the continent: cut-priced excursions for large, organised groups, they brought exotic destinations

13-14 LONG ACRE IN 1880

ABOVE: **The Long Acre façade in 1880, before its enlargement; the carriages in the adjoining shops are a reminder that Long Acre was once famous for its carriage-makers, and later for its car showrooms.**

23

ABOVE: **Cockspur Street in 1890 –
the Stanford façade just visible on
the left.**

within the reach of thousands of people, and gave a huge impetus to tourism – itself a new word and new concept in the English language. From the first, Stanford sold geographical books and guides, for the "tourist", for the elderly visitor to Madeira, the energetic Alpinist, the yachtsman bound for the Mediterranean or the lady visiting India. It seems clear that the world of maps was at this time essentially the male world: the world of the military and the navy, the government and the administrators, the explorers and scientists, the clubs and the committees. Tourism formed the exception to this rule, a form of travel in which women could participate, and if female mapmakers were unknown, many guide books and travel narratives were written by women.

So this was the context in which Edward Stanford began to develop his business. He became the intermediary between official map sources and the general public. He had the vision to appreciate the wealth of topographical information that was available in official survey maps, and the energy to recycle it into commercial form. From being a mere map shop, he transformed his business into "Stanford's Geographical Establishment".

Stanford's earliest maps, such as those of Sebastapol or of Canterbury, were of limited or ephemeral interest, and he recognised that to establish himself as a serious force in the map world he must produce maps of more universal appeal, and replace the ageing S.D.U.K. maps which he had acquired. With the help of Trelawney Saunders therefore, he conceived and published the series of "Library Maps", obviously intended to be competition-killers. These were to be huge, spectacular and highly detailed maps of the world and the six continents, designed for display on the walls of libraries, business offices and government departments. They were each printed in four sheets, to be assembled into one large map, twenty-five square feet in size. Already in 1857, Stanford had published an impressive two-sheet map of India, perhaps intended as a trial-run for the Library Maps. Europe was the first of the Library Maps to appear in 1858, followed by Australasia in 1859, Asia in 1862, North America in 1863, South America in 1864, with Africa completing the set in 1866. Strangely perhaps, the Library Map of the World did not appear until 1879. Stanford recognised that these maps would require frequent updating: the first edition of Africa inevitably shows a huge blank area in the centre, although Stanford could scarcely have foreseen the dramatic political changes which would render the first Europe edition obsolete. It is for precisely these reasons that these maps are now of outstanding interest to the historian, showing as they do both the progress of exploration and the forces of political change. Saunders acted as editor for these maps, and they were drawn by A. Keith Johnston of Edinburgh, probably the best cartographic draughtsman in Britain. Johnston worked for other mapmakers including Bartholomew, but he clearly enjoyed a close relationship with Stanford, and his son, also Keith Johnston, worked for Stanford in 1866–67 (this younger Johnston died in 1879 during an expedition to Africa). The Library Maps were engraved by Johnston on copper plates and printed in the traditional manner, while the additional colours showing seas, rivers and political divisions were added by hand-colourists, working in the traditional way with watercolours. The combined talents of Saunders, Johnston and Stanford produced in these Library Maps outstanding examples of nineteenth-century cartography, which, if Stanford had published nothing else, would have secured him a place in the history of mapmaking. In 1862 a Library Map of London was a milestone in the mapmaking of the capital because it was the first to make use of the recently completed large-scale Ordnance survey of London. This survey had been carried out at the massive scale of 60 inches to one mile (the so called five-foot plan) and was published in outline form in 400 sheets, which were of course of little use to the general public. With immense labour, Saunders reduced this material to twenty-four sheets and created by far the best map available of Victorian London.

These large maps could be bought as plain paper sheets of course, but from the outset Stanford added value to them by offering them in a variety of mountings. They could be assembled into one large sheet, backed on strong linen, and varnished for wall display, or they could be dissected into

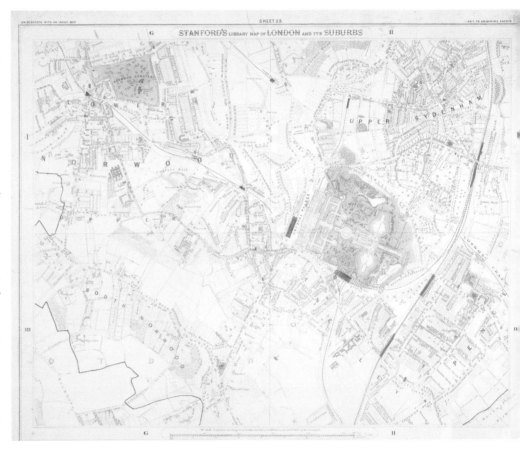

BELOW: **A section of Stanford's *Library Map of London* 1862, showing Crystal Palace.**

sections the size of an average book, and folded into a handsome leather case, which would then take its place on a bookshelf. These mountings ensured that maps would survive many years of regular use. The map mounting section was one of the five main departments into which the business came naturally to be divided: the public saw the map showroom, but behind the scenes there was the Ordnance Survey map depot, the cartographic drawing office, the printing works and the mounting room.

By 1860 Stanford was also developing his business in two other important directions: he began publishing books on geographical and related subjects, and he undertook cartographic work for other publishers. His earliest books were not guidebooks, but were descriptive accounts of regions such as Canada, Southern Africa or New Zealand, aimed either at potential emigrants or at the "missionary market". In the first category was *New Zealand, the Britain of the South* by Charles Hursthouse, and in the second *The Kafirs of Natal and the Zulu Country* by the Reverend James Shooter, "lately a missionary in Natal". From these modest beginnings, Stanford would, in the following thirty years, build an extensive list of books whose titles indicate the ever widening connections which geography was making with other aspects of Victorian experience. There were books on military and naval subjects; on political and historical subjects, especially colonial affairs; on certain sciences such as geology and astronomy; on a wide range of educational subjects; on the history of exploration and mapmaking; and descriptive geographical books on every region of the world, from the lochs of Scotland to the Trans-Siberian railway. However, one important point has to be made about Stanford's book-publishing: from the outset a great deal of it was commission publishing, a system in which the author paid for all or part of the expenses of the publication, and the profits were shared between author and publisher. Stanford would produce the book, and his imprint was on it; he would advertise and distribute it to the book trade, but the author had guaranteed him against loss by his advance payment. An account was kept for each title, and when its sales revenue passed the amount of the guarantee, the author would begin to earn a profit. The defects of this arrangement compared with the normal system of risk publishing are obvious: if the publisher is guaranteed against loss, he will be less discriminating than perhaps he should be about which manuscripts to accept, and he will make less effort than he should to sell the book. It would be wrong to suppose that the commission system meant that Stanford would publish anything simply for a fee, since profit was still the aim, and his name would be on the book, contributing to his reputation. But it cannot be claimed that his book publishing programme compared in quality with that of the leading publishing houses such as John Murray, Longman or Macmillan. The commission system explains why the range of Stanford's books appears to become so wide, and increasingly whimsical – *The Life and Traditions of the Canadian Beaver, The*

Floating Island in Derwentwater or *How to Pack, Dress and Keep Well on a Winter Tour in India* would hardly threaten the supremacy of those other publishers.

But perhaps those publishers and Stanford were content with this hierarchy, in view of the cartographic services which he could offer them for their own books. Books of travel, history and geography had to be illustrated, and John Murray and many others turned naturally to Stanford to provide maps, which would be folded and bound in with the book. One of the earliest of these maps was provided in 1857 for Murray's *Letters from High Latitudes ...a Voyage.. to Iceland, Jan Mayen and Spitzbergen* by Lord Dufferin, later Governor-General of Canada and then Viceroy of India. Subsequently Stanford would draw maps for many important books, by Edward Whymper, by Heinrich Schliemann and by Francis Younghusband. Stanford enjoyed good relations with Murray, and we know that Murray sent many manuscripts to Stanford which he could not accept as risk publications, while Stanford in turn advised authors unwilling to accept commission terms to go to Murray.

In all his cartographic activity Stanford's business was enormously strengthened by the talents of John Bolton, a man who was to make a major contribution to the firm. Like Edward Stanford himself, Bolton had little formal education, and joined Stanford in 1858 as a boy of fourteen. He was still working part-time at his death in 1925 after an extraordinary sixty-seven years' service, during which time he became Stanford's chief cartographer, a Fellow of the R.G.S. and an acknowledged expert on geography who was consulted by individuals such as General Gordon, H.M. Stanley and Frederick Lugard, as well as by the British government, who took him as a special adviser to the Berlin Congress in 1878. In the 1920s young Stanford employees were taught to revere Bolton as "the man who defied Bismarck", although what exactly he said to the Iron Chancellor is sadly lost to history. It seems unlikely to have been a volcanic confrontation, since Bolton was invariably described as a genial, modest figure, regarded with affection by everyone with whom he worked. John Bolton was twice married, the second time in 1907 at the age of sixty-three, when Stanford noted that Mr. Bolton absented himself for "a short honeymoon". Bolton had personal correspondence with all Stanford's cartographic clients, most notably perhaps with H.M. Stanley. During their first contacts in 1878, when Stanley had just returned from his historic first journey down the Congo, the egotistical explorer launched a fierce attack on armchair mapmakers. "I see how African geography is so much misunderstood," he wrote, "and that it is due entirely to you mapmakers. It is to Stanford's establishment I attribute the loss of Frank Pocock and at least thirteen others who were drowned … Maps are veritable death-traps to travellers." Bolton must indeed have returned a soft answer to this extraordinary claim, for all Stanley's subsequent letters took a very different tone, full of increasing respect and friendship,

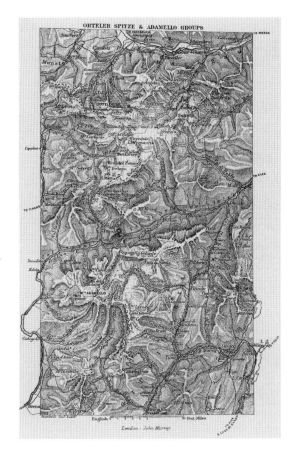

ABOVE: **The Ortler and Adamello peaks from Murray's** *Handbook to Southern Germany and Austria,* **typical of the maps which Stanford drew for John Murray during the 1880s and 1890s.**
The Bodleian Library

as Bolton helped him construct maps recording his African journeys. Five years before his death Stanley paid Bolton his highest compliment when he wrote to him, "Had it not been my fate to have been an African explorer, I should have wished to be a geographer of your attainments." Another eccentric genius who had reason to be grateful to John Bolton was the novelist Samuel Butler, whom Bolton helped to construct a map of Homeric geography, to illustrate Butler's bizarre theory that Homer had been in reality a woman and a native of Sicily. Sadly, very few of Bolton's working papers have survived, but it is tempting to see him as the successor to Trelawney Saunders, in providing Stanford with the outstanding level of geographical expertise essential to the business, and to which Stanford himself made no pretence. Bolton's expertise was essential when the commission publishing system was applied to maps. An explorer or missionary or mining prospector returning to London with new topographic information would frequently approach Stanford to publish his findings in a new map. Just as with the books, an agreement about shared costs and profits would be reached, and John Bolton's department would work up the client's drawings into a finished map, which Stanford would publish and sell. It is usually possible to identify these maps from Stanford's catalogues since they are described as compiled or prepared by a named individual. Stanford was especially busy on such maps of the Transvaal gold-bearing region in the 1890s, when many surveyors saw the opportunity to market their special knowledge.

As Stanford's business grew rapidly in the 1860s, he acquired additional space by taking over numbers 7 and 8 Charing Cross, partly to house the enormous stock of Ordnance Survey maps. In was in 1874 that the first of several changes of location were forced on the firm, for in that year the Metropolitan Board of Works (the forerunner of the London County Council) compulsorily purchased 6, 7 and 8 Charing Cross for demolition connected with the opening of Northumberland Avenue. Stanford quickly found new premises at 55 Charing Cross, where he opened his showroom. This was opposite the original shop, on the west side of modern Whitehall, where the Admiralty Arch now stands. But this site was not large enough for the whole business, even though adjoining space at numbers 54 and 56 were soon added, so the printing and cartographic works were separated and moved into their own offices some way off, at numbers 13 and 14 Long Acre. In the era before telephones the quarter-mile which separated the two sites caused endless difficulties. By this time, the mid-1870s, Stanford himself no longer lived at his business premises, but had moved into a substantial villa in the London suburb of Bromley, where his son was to grow up. In 1888 the Board of Works again stepped in, requiring the new site for more road development, this time the extension from the Mall which would open out into Trafalgar Square. It was now the second Edward Stanford who was compelled to move again a short distance to 26-27 Cockspur Street, and he

OPPOSITE: **John Bolton, Stanford's chief cartographer for over fifty years, and one of the maps which he drew to illustrate the African journeys of H.M. Stanley.**
The Royal Geographical Society/The British Library

noticed bitterly that the new street, for which he was forced to move, was still not built at the turn of the century, and in fact it did not finally appear until 1910 when it was made to pass beneath the new Admiralty Arch. The Cockspur Street building was given a fine new façade, which still survives, on which globes and figures of Atlas were carved in stone. This was still not the end of Stanford's wandering, however, for in 1899 the London County Council began negotiating to acquire the Cockspur Street site for its own offices. By this time the difficulties of having his business split between two sites had become so irritating that Stanford was ready to sell. He decided to enlarge the Long Acre premises and reunite all the firm's activities under one roof, and in 1901 the final move to 12, 13 and 14 Long Acre took place, even though, confusingly, he still maintained a second showroom at Cockspur Street until 1905. In the thirty years between 1873 and 1903 Stanford publications can show one of four addresses: 6 Charing Cross, 55 Charing Cross, Cockspur Street or Long Acre. The fine Dutch-gable façade of the Long Acre building was designed by the architect Herbert Read, a close friend of Stanford's, and is still a landmark. On arriving in the new building Stanford acquired his first typewriter and his first telephone. The determination to remain within the firm's original heartland was obviously strong through all these moves, and the move to Long Acre was viewed at first with some doubt, for Covent Garden was then seen as a far less promising area for such a business. In one respect however he may have been glad to leave Trafalgar Square, which, then as now, was the scene of many public meetings, sometimes violent, for in October 1892 Stanford recorded with disgust that the windows of the Cockspur Street showroom had been smashed by a mob.

In 1874, shortly before this period of upheavals had begun, Stanford had made a purchase which was to be of the greatest importance for his future publishing. He acquired the copper plates of John Arrowsmith's *London Atlas of Universal Geography,* a work which had appeared in various editions between 1834 and 1860, and which was generally regarded as the finest international atlas published in England. Arrowsmith was now dead, and the purchase of these plates suggests that Stanford was planning to crown his publishing programme by producing a comprehensive international atlas. To produce such a work entirely from original sources would be virtually impossible, and the availability of the Arrowsmith plates gave him the basis he needed. Even so a further fifteen years' work would be required before the appearance in 1887 of the magnificent folio edition of *Stanford's London Atlas of Universal Geography.*

Edward Stanford senior had suffered for many years from chronic asthma, and had planned for some time to retire in favour of his son. This transfer occurred officially in January 1882, when Edward Stanford junior became head of the firm, although the father maintained part-time contact until 1885. Although we know little of what the former was really like, we can infer several important facts. Without

ABOVE: **The second Edward Stanford, under whom the firm enjoyed its golden age.**

formal education, he undoubtedly possessed enormous vision and energy to sense the commercial potential of the map market in nineteenth-century London, and to take possession of it so successfully. The 1881 census shows Stanford employing eighty-seven staff, and no one would then have disputed that for international maps, Ordnance Survey maps and geographical books, Stanfords was supreme in London. His personality impressed everyone who dealt with him, and inspired official mapping agencies with the confidence to cooperate with him. He harnessed the talents of Trelawney Saunders, John Bolton, A. Keith Johnston, and many others to create a business whose commercial and technical foundations were first-class. He continued to live in London until 1890, when he retired to Sidmouth in Devon. In his last years, his illness made life a burden to him, and he died in November 1904 at the age of seventy-eight.

It was during the years 1885 to 1910 under the direction of his son, that Stanfords enjoyed its golden age, and that its name became pre-eminent throughout the English-speaking world as a map publisher and map seller. It happens that we know far more in this period about the working of the firm and about the man himself through the chance survival of a number of revealing documents, both professional and personal. The records are by no means complete, and there are many questions which can probably never be answered, but a richer and more human picture emerges of the life of a Victorian house of business. The second Edward Stanford was born in 1856 at the premises in 6 Charing Cross, but his upbringing was significantly different from his father's. He was sent to Uppingham public school, and then studied at Marburg University and in Paris, and although he seems not to have taken a formal degree, he became proficient in German and French. It was not unusual for the sons of Victorian men of business to study abroad, and it certainly suggests that he was destined to follow in his father's footsteps. Mild and thoughtful-looking in a youthful photograph, later portraits show him as a formidable autocrat, with a regal Edwardian beard and a masterful gaze. For thirty years this man ruled his "house" with an unyielding hand, leaving both his staff and his clients in no doubt that Stanfords was no mere business, but a service for gentlemen governed by one who was very much their equal. Given John Bolton's expertise as a pure map maker, it was natural that when Stanford succeeded his father he should leave the "geographical department" in Bolton's hands, while he himself took charge of the book publishing programme, keeping control of course of all the strategic policy decisions, for example those concerned with the Ordnance Survey or the Hydrographic Office. He was frequently asked by the Colonial Office to sell the official maps of various colonies, and he cooperated with the War Office as a contract publisher. In fact the War Office came to rely on Stanfords fulfilling this role to such an extent that they tried to steer him towards publishing major works of military reference for them, which Stanford declined to do.

OVER PAGE: **Inside the newly-opened Long Acre showroom and the cartographic drawing office in 1901.**

The jewels in the crown of Stanford's publishing programme had both been initiated by Edward Stanford the elder, but they were brought to fruition by his son: these were *Stanford's London Atlas of Universal Geography* and *Stanford's Compendium of Geography and Travel*. The atlas appeared as a large folio in 1887, dedicated to Queen Victoria in her Golden Jubilee year. Approximately half of its contents of ninety maps was based on the Arrowsmith plates acquired in 1873. These had been up dated of course, and the list included general small-scale maps of France, Europe, Asia, the United States and so on, as well as some more unusual maps such as "The Acquisitions of Russia since the Accession of Peter the Great", a map which provides clear evidence of Britain's suspicions about Russian policy. The other half of the atlas consisted of new maps, some of them such as Cyprus, Palestine, the Cape Colony and Jamaica based on large-scale survey maps which Stanford had already published. India, Canada, Australia and Africa were strongly represented by high-quality regional maps. Oddities included a map of the environs of Troy in western Turkey, clearly derived too from a survey which Stanford had published, and a detailed chart of the Falkland Islands. The sheet maps which were used to make up this atlas were also sold separately, and they were kept up to date on an individual basis. At this period when the binding of a large book like this was carried out expensively by hand, it was the practice for publishers to bind up only a small number of copies at one time, the bulk of the stock being stored in quires. As a result of this practice and as a result of the up dating of individual maps, any two copies of this atlas are unlikely to be identical in every detail, in spite of sharing the same title page – a source of confusion to modern bibliographers and collectors. Stanford defended this practice – of having many maps more recent than the atlas's title page – as being far more desirable than the practice of most other publishers, which was to up date the title page year by year, while leaving the maps unchanged and out-of-date. New editions of this atlas with substantially altered and enlarged contents appeared in 1893 and in 1904, the latter now containing 110 maps. The whole production was widely regarded as the finest world atlas available in England at the time, the *Daily Telegraph* crowning its review with the judgement that the maps were "a credit not only to Mr. Stanford but to British cartography … there is no atlas to surpass the *London Atlas* in the entire world." Was it a coincidence that Stanford received a royal warrant as cartographer to the Queen in 1893, after he had written in his preface that "many new and original maps, critically drawn and engraved, have been added, especially for the sake of more completely representing the British Empire"?

Stanford's Compendium of Geography and Travel was planned as a fundamental reference resource, offering descriptions of the geography and the peoples of the entire world, continent by continent. It has a strong claim to be considered the first encyclopedia of world geography to be published in English. As a

33

OPPOSITE: **The map printing-press in 1901.**

work of reference it was intended to take the Stanford name into all the best libraries, public and private, and to function as a textual counterpart to the great atlas. Stanford acknowledged as his model for this series a German work called *Die Erde und ihre Völker,* by Friedrich Hellwald, which Stanford had surely read during his stay in Germany. It was a serial publication issued in Stuttgart in fifty parts during the 1870s, but it has a decidedly populist look, and it is hard to see exactly what Stanford took from it except the general idea of a geographical encyclopedia in many volumes. Hellwald's work was illustrated with numerous small woodcuts, but contained no maps, and it was not even organised into continental volumes, as Stanford's was. No doubt it was used by Stanford as a general source book, but it was almost entirely rewritten by a team of geographical authors who were first-rate, or nearly so. The general editor and author of half the volumes was Augustus Henry Keane, a writer whose fortunes were closely linked to Stanford's for thirty years.

Keane was born in Cork in 1833 and educated sporadically in Dublin, Italy and Germany, before travelling through Europe and the Americas. He was evidently a fine linguist, became an "ethnologist", or as we should now call it an anthropologist, a fellow of the Royal Geographical Society and, somehow, Professor of Hindustani at University College, London, although he seems never to have visited India or to have published on the subject. He always described himself simply as "a hard-working literary man", and he unquestionably worked hard for Stanford on these massive volumes and on a number of other monographs. Other famous authors who helped to produce the *Compendium* included Alfred Russell Wallace, Sir Clements Markham, Keith Johnston the younger, E.G. Ravenstein, and H.W. Bates, the South American explorer. Less well known today were many university professors such as George Chisholm, A.R.C. Selwyn, and F.V. Hayden, while Henry Gannett was head of the United States Geological Survey. The series began with *Africa* in 1878 and reached completion in 1885 with *Europe.* Each volume went through several printings, often revised and corrected by other writers, and by the early 1890s Stanford was preparing a completely new edition, giving two volumes to each continent, a programme which reached completion with the second volume of *Europe* in 1902. These new editions often had new authors, and some were edited by the indefatigable Keane; the result is a rather complex publishing history in which, as with the atlas, two copies of apparently the same title may not be identical. Poor Keane worked so furiously on this series of books that just before Christmas of 1898 his doctor wrote indignantly to Stanford demanding that he allow his patient some rest. A slightly chastened Stanford wrote Keane a sympathetic note in response, but still enclosed some further proofs for correction! The twelve volumes were rounded off by a glossary of geographical terms compiled by Alexander Knox of the War Office Geographical Staff.

With its uniform green and gold bindings embossed with the motifs of the continents from the Albert Memorial, and with its Eurocentric perspective, the *Compendium* seems to embody a confident statement of Victorian geographical knowledge, of the belief that the world was rapidly yielding up its secrets to scientific study whose definitive results could be found in these solid, reassuring volumes.

The *Compendium* was Stanford's most ambitious risk publication, but he had many other distinguished and successful books, among all the commission work. There were political books by J. Scott Keltie, Secretary of the R.G.S.; geographical textbooks by Keith Johnston the younger; geological works by authors such as Sir Andrew Ramsay, James Geikie and Edward Hull; and the delightful illustrated works of popular science by Arabella Buckley, whose titles such as *The Fairyland of Science* sold in their thousands. If many of the commission books are distinctly forgettable, others were important and worthwhile. *The Evolution of Geography,* 1899, by John Keane (not discoverably related to A.H. Keane) is a readable and accurate history of exploration and discovery from classical times to the voyage of Magellan. One of the strengths of this little book is the attractive series of maps copied from ancient and medieval sources, for which Keane thanks John Bolton in his preface. Many of these Stanford books of course were distinguished by precisely drawn maps, produced by Bolton's department. Another risk series which Stanford developed was his little "Two-Shilling Guides" to the counties and regions of Britain, whose authors were often country clergymen, some of whom had some slight distinction as authors – P.H. Ditchfield and R.N. Worth for example. Dull looking by modern standards, they were thoughtful, literate guides suited to their time, and their pocket format caused them to be praised by the *Saturday Review* as "indispensable for the pedestrian, horseman and bicyclist … nearly as light and twice as portable as a fairly well-filled cigar-case".

With all its huge range of military, geographical, descriptive and semi-scientific works, Stanford's book-publishing conspicuously lacked a series of international guidebooks, and in 1901 he took a major plunge and acquired one, by purchasing the famous John Murray *Handbooks.* These books were the original, the matchless, travelguides of the high Victorian age. From the English Channel to the shores of Asia, to be seen in possession of one's Murray in a train, on board ship, or in the hotel foyer, was to be marked out as a serious, literate and well-prepared traveller. The series had been initiated in 1836, the early volumes written personally by John Murray II, regularly revised or rewritten by expert authors, but always published anonymously. When Stanford bought the series for £2,000 in 1901 he must have believed that he had joined the major league in the book publishing world; however he was soon to be disillusioned. Within a year of the transaction he had discovered that there was insufficient stock of the maps to bind into the books, and he had to negotiate with Murray to share the cost of many map reprints. This undermined all his calculations of the value of the books, and strained his friendship with Murray. Secondly he had underestimated the impact which newer guide series, especially the Baedekers, had had on the sales of the Murrays. But thirdly, and most important, he was quite unprepared for the time and effort involved in up-dating the guides. New railways were being built, new buildings and streets appeared in cities while old ones were demolished, hotels came and went, political events altered the psychological landscape, archaeological discoveries uncovered new sites to visit, and so on. Authors who had spent years researching their books were often unwilling to be told they must rewrite for a fresh edition, and new authors had to be recruited. Stanford was driven to retain a full-time editor, John Manson, to handle the series for him, but he could not escape the difficult financial decisions about rewriting the books, and he was shocked when, for example, he was told in 1903 by an Egyptologist from the British Museum that the book on Egypt needed to be entirely rewritten by an expert. By 1905 he was letting it be known that he was willing to resell the series if a buyer could be found. Nevertheless Stanford's management of the *Handbooks* had some highlights: for example the new book on Switzerland which he commissioned from the famous Alpinist W.A.B. Coolidge was highly praised.

One of Stanford's major preoccupations during his entire period as head of the firm was naturally with the Ordnance Survey. A large proportion of his premises was taken up with storing the hundreds of thousands of sheets of the six-inch and twenty-five-inch maps, and their steadily increasing sale was one of the foundations of his business. He went to great lengths to promote their sale, issuing his own detailed catalogues and advertising his services extensively in the press. But the Survey was restless in its dealings with the commercial map trade, and made frequent changes in their terms and contracts with Stanford. Sometimes this worked to his advantage, sometimes it worked against him, but the changes almost invariably produced stress and weariness. The high point in Stanford's relationship with the Survey came in 1885 when he was appointed sole agent for England and Wales, that is all Ordnance Survey maps sold to the public or to other retail outlets passed through his hands. He received 33⅓% discount on the published price, and gave 25% discount in turn to other retailers. This was a trial scheme for one year, and in 1886 tenders were invited from other map sellers to offer a premium for fulfilling this role. Stanford's offer of an annual premium of £600 was accepted, and his sole agency was to last for a further twelve years. Separate agencies were appointed in Edinburgh and Dublin. This was the period when the Stanford name became synonymous with the Ordnance Survey, and there is no doubt that considerable resentment was felt in the retail map trade at being compelled to buy from a trade rival.

Dec 17th.   13

Scott's Last Expedition.

Messrs Smith Elder & Co.,
     15, Waterloo Place.
             S.W.

Dear Sirs,
     We feel we cannot let your advertisement in to-day's
"Times" pass without a word of thanks for the mention of our
firm as the map-makers for the above book. It is such an
unusual thing for co-workers to be mentioned (except in prefaces)
that we thank you all the more heartily for the worldwide
publicity which you are giving us all to-day. That the book
must be a success was undoubted from the first, owing to the
heart-rending pathos of the story, and we are all proud to
have our names associated with it, however little we may have
done to help that success. We should like to congratulate you
on the tout ensemble of the book, and to thank Lady Scott
for allowing the diaries to be made public.

          With renewed thanks ,
               We are, dear Sirs,
                    Yours faithfully
                         Edward Stanford, Ltd.,
                              Governing Director.

                    Edward Stanford

ABOVE: **A typical extract from Edward Stanford's letter-books; this one, dated December 1913, concerns a map drawn in connection with Scott's last expedition.**

In the early 1890s, however, the Ordnance Survey maps began to be subject to a growing tide of criticism. Professional users pointed out that many of the maps were twenty or thirty years out of date, and therefore did not show crucially important new features such as railways. There were many other points of criticism, including price and availability. The result was several years' work by committees of enquiry which looked at the whole Ordnance Survey enterprise and the service which it was supposed to be giving to the public. Edward Stanford was naturally among those who were called to give evidence, and he took the opportunity to describe the difficulties and costs of selling such a complex multi-sheet series to the public. He was particularly incensed by the Director-General himself, Sir Charles Wilson, who had stated publicly that Stanford was being "rewarded" with his 33⅓% discount simply for handing maps over to the public. Stanford pointed out that a large proportion of his sales was to the trade, at a gross profit of only 8%, and that he must pay building, staff and postal costs, not to mention his annual premium of £600. So strong were his feelings that he made his only venture into print on this subject in 1891, with a pamphlet entitled *The Ordnance Survey from a Business Point of View*. Nevertheless Wilson's opposition to the sole agency system prevailed, supported by claims from other map sellers that their businesses were tending to be regarded as second-rate because they could not obtain Ordnance maps direct, as Stanford could. In 1897 a change of policy gave Stanford the sole agency only for London and only for sales to the public, while the Survey resumed direct sales to other book and map sellers. Stanford was to hold credit stock of all sheets of England and Wales, paying the Survey once each quarter for the maps he had sold. Stanford undoubtedly knew that he was losing valuable business: he later recorded that between 1885 and 1905 the value of his sales of Ordnance maps totalled almost £300,000, yielding him a gross profit of almost £80,000. In those days of low wages this represented an enviable level of income, and of course Stanford's business was entirely his own: its profits were his to spend, and he spent very freely and lived very well. We know that at this time John Bolton's salary was a mere £300 per year, while a reasonable estimate would suggest that Edward Stanford's own annual income was at least ten times that figure.

Our insight into Stanford as a personality and into the nature of his business is much richer in this period because of the survival of a long, but not quite complete, series of letters from 1892 to 1917. Some of his correspondents were famous men of their era – Edward Whymper, Captain Scott, Alfred Russel Wallace, Ernest Shackleton, Sir Clements Markham, Francis Younghusband, John Murray – while others were important in the more limited affairs of Stanfords itself – his *Compendium* authors, officials of the Ordnance Survey or the Publishers Association, or other map sellers such as Bartholomew and Philip. It is frustrating that, except in very rare cases, we have only one side of the correspondence, and therefore have to infer what Stanford is responding to. Few of these letters are individually startling or revelatory, but taken together they build up an intriguing picture of a Victorian man of business. In these letters Stanford is undoubtedly acting a well rehearsed role: dignified, magisterial, correct, he nevertheless takes delight in revealing that he is no mere tradesman. He became expert at parrying the attacks of insolent customers, resentful trade rivals, egotistical authors and tedious officials. You sense that here is a man holding himself in, compelled to use the formal language of business, but hinting that he too is acquainted with the pleasures of travelling, dining or weekend shooting, when the tedious ritual of business is finished.

Like most publishers he spent a large slice of his time fending off would-be authors, breaking the news to them that their schemes for maps printed on handkerchiefs, books on ice skating techniques, on bicycling in Norway, or the birds of Rutland failed to excite him. To belligerent customers he explained endlessly that he merely sold Ordnance maps, and was not responsible for their accuracy or their price, or the time taken by the Post Office to deliver them. Weekly if not daily, he had to chase bad debts, pointing out to imperious baronets or wrathful army officers that no business can survive if it does not collect what it is owed. One of the most striking lessons of these letters is the universality of credit in nineteenth-century England: anyone with a readable handwriting and a plausible address could apparently send for maps, and receive them with a bill, knowing that six months would probably elapse before he would be called upon to pay. If he were an officer or a peer, goods might be sent to India or South Africa, and years would pass before Stanford ventured to press for payment. He hears himself called a "damned dunning tradesman" for requesting the favour of a cheque for maps sent out a year ago. But Stanford was usually equal to the conflict, once observing acidly that by some people even "truth is apt to be considered discourtesy", and he once reminded a supercilious Bishop that there could be "only one judge of how Mr. Stanford's business should be conducted". In extreme cases he was known to return a customer's insolent letter with his order, and decline icily to deal with him at all. He was undoubtedly a sucker for an aristocratic title, but an incident in the Long Acre shop with the arrogant Lord Ronald Sutherland Gower made him write to John Murray "The days of whispering breath and bated humbleness to anyone with a title (because of the title) are I hope passed. I am a Conservative, but such treatment of 'underlings' is a cause of, and excuse for, Socialism." All this was part of the inevitable guerrilla warfare that is retailing, where staff and customers collide. On a more serious level, there are letters of genuine historical interest. In October 1907, Captain Robert Falcon Scott wrote to him:

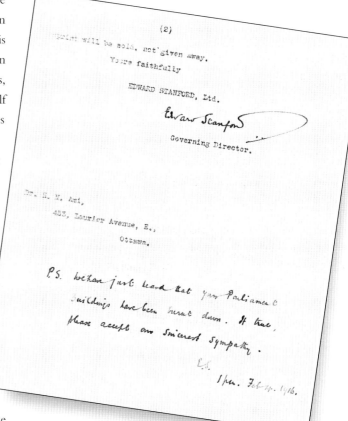

ABOVE: **A letter from Edward Stanford to his Canadian author, Dr. H.M. Ami, with an intriguing postscript on the burning of the Canadian parliament in February, 1916 – "P.S. We have just heard that your Parliament buildings have been burnt down. If true, please accept our sincerest sympathy."**

56, OAKLEY STREET,
CHELSEA EMBANKMENT.

ABOVE: **Letter from Captain Scott, October 1907, complaining about Stanford's map of the Antarctic.**

"Sir,

I have just received your map of the Antarctic Regions (London Atlas Series) and I observe that the farthest point south is marked 'Scott and Shackleton', an inscription which is not in accordance with any authoritative map published by the Geographical Society but which is naturally one of the most interesting in the map.

According to all precedent, this coupling of Mr. Shackelton's name with mine implies dual leadership, and it is therefore not in accordance with fact.

Mr. Shackelton's name cannot have been added by you with a wish to note this whole party which reached the farthest point, since the name of Wilson is omitted.

In view of these remarks I wish to ask your authority for the inscription and your purpose in making it.

I remain

Yours faithfully

R.F.Scott

Captain R.N.

Late *Discovery* "

To this touchy letter Stanford replied with dignity:

"Dear Captain Scott,

I have your letter of the 16th, and I am exceedingly sorry to find that you take exception that at the furthest point south your name is coupled with Lieut. Shackleton's. That wording was inserted in the year 1903, before anything authoritative was issued, and your book was not issued until two years later. My authority for the 'inscription' was the then known facts as reported in the press and elsewhere, and I had no special 'purpose' in making it. In my opinion, no inference of 'dual leadership' should be drawn from the wording. Everybody knew that you were the leader of the *Discovery* expedition. I had the pleasure of sending you an early proof of this very map in July 1901 when you were starting, and also the pleasure of dining with you after your return. However if you wish, I will omit Lieut. Shackleton's name in the next printing. I see since 1903 it has been added to the plate at Shackleton Inlet, in the same way that the other officers' names are perpetuated on the map.

May I say that personally I had no knowledge of the wording on the map, although I am, of course, responsible for it?

> Yours faithfully
>
> Edward Stanford"

This seems to have soothed Scott's ego, and his tone changed noticeably when he realised that Stanford was obviously a man of education and breeding:

"Dear Mr. Stanford,

I must thank you for your courteous reply to my hasty letter and apologise unreservedly for suggesting that there might be a purpose in the inscription to which I took exception.

I clearly see from your letter how this mistake arose and hasten to express my regret for my last letter …

… I tried to be impartial in giving credit to my companions who one and all laboured honestly and well as I have endeavoured to record – I grow hot at this idea of one being advertised at the expense of his fellows – I trust you will consider this my excuse for my first letter …

… I understand now of course that you had no personal knowledge of the wording and I must express regret that I failed to realise your identity when I first wrote.

> Believe me
>
> Yours faithfully
>
> R.F. Scott"

In this exchange, Stanford was the peacemaker, but his correspondence reveals that he could be prickly in defence of his reputation, or where his own commercial interests were concerned. In September 1885 he became involved in a dispute with J.D. Potter the Admiralty Chart agent from whom Stanford bought his chart stock, because Potter would not take back some outdated charts for credit. Stanford appealed to the Admiralty, who wisely declined to become involved, and Stanford angrily threw up his sub-agency for Admiralty charts, although he later restored it not because it created any great profit but because its loss diminished the range of his business. In his complaint to the Hydrographic Office he commented, "About forty years ago a sub-agency for Admiralty Charts was taken by this house, then under Mr.

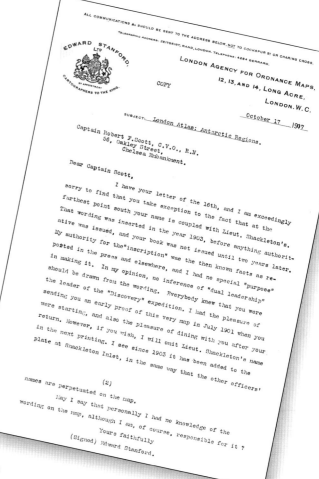

ABOVE: **Stanford's reply to Scott.**

Trelawney Saunders, for the convenience of the yachting members of both Houses of Parliament. This agency has been carried on ever since by my father and myself … I am not anxious to break a connection which has existed so long." In 1904 he initiated a quarrel with the Scottish map fraternity when he interpreted some remarks in the *Scottish Geographical Magazine* as suggesting that he had taken some Bartholomew maps, revised them, and added his own name to them. The issue concerned maps drawn by Bartholomew for one of the Murray *Handbooks*: when Stanford bought those books, he bought the maps that went with them, and considered that he had the right to revise them and add his imprint to them. The quarrel dragged on for months, and Stanford threatened to sever all connection with the *Magazine* and with the Edinburgh mapping establishment, but was finally mollified by a printed retraction.

These letters occasionally reveal unexpected matters of personal interest, for example it emerges that Stanford had a younger half-brother named William, some fifteen years his junior, the child of his father's second marriage. William worked in the business, but evidently not in any senior capacity, and by 1903 he had left and had set himself up in a rival map business, based in Oxford. This business soon foundered, and Stanford himself bought up the stock and interest, while William returned to London to become manager of G. W. Bacon's map shop. Edward Stanford mentioned to more than one correspondent that his father had been pained by William's actions, and that William had eventually to be legally barred from trading under the Stanford name. One can only speculate whether some deep family quarrel lay behind these strange events.

Unexpectedly perhaps, these letters have their comic side. In 1898 Stanford bought a quantity of old atlases from Chapman and Hall, the well-known publisher, but on examining them he wrote to complain that some of them had clearly been used for target practice with a rifle. "I enclose," he added sarcastically, "the bullet." In 1897, Edward Aveling, translator and son-in-law of Karl Marx, wrote asking for a free copy of Stanford's great *London Atlas* in return for puffing it in a preface. Stanford explained loftily that his *Atlas* was a work "whose nature precludes gratuitous distribution", and he returned the proofs of Marx's work unread. In 1899 he had to reassure Keane that Sir Clements Markham's criticisms of one of Keane's books was not desperately serious. "The relation of criticisms to the work," he wrote, "bears the same proportion as Falstaff's bread to his sack." Perhaps most bizarre of all, he complained to a correspondent that her friend had caused him a great deal of trouble by committing suicide in Stanford's offices. The dead man had evidently been an employee, but Stanford argued that he had always been well-treated, and had no possible excuse for his "rash act". Just occasionally he unbends and gives vent to his feelings of frustration at the petty tyranny of business life. Complaining to one old and valued client, he wrote of the "constant grinding down" of "mean business" practices, and he exclaimed that, "So long as I can, I will act on my own independent lines, and when my business fails me in consequence, a good crossing like that at the Athenaeum Club may have to be swept by Yours faithfully, Edward Stanford." Like Mr. Lorry in *A Tale of Two Cities,* Stanford might have exclaimed "Feelings! I have no time for them, no chance of them. I pass my whole life in turning an immense pecuniary mangle."

All this stress and indignity was the price Stanford paid for his growing success and wealth. These are both reflected in another group of documents which have miraculously survived, his personal account books, which record virtually every penny of personal expenditure during the 1880s and 1890s. From these books, spare and apparently impersonal as they are, there emerges a rich and detailed picture of this man's private life: his holidays in Brighton or on the Continent, his gifts of flowers for his wife Caroline, his new top hats and new tennis rackets, his lunches at Kettner's restaurant, his shopping at Fortnum's, Lillywhite's or the Army and Navy Stores. He had inherited from his father a large house in the London suburb of Bromley, but he also bought a country house at Aldringham, on the Suffolk coast where he enjoyed weekend shooting, and he maintained a flat in Kensington. He took holidays in the Norwegian fjords and in Switzerland, or cruised the Mediterranean and visited Egypt and the Holy Land. His three sons were all sent to public schools – Uppingham or Rugby – and he invested in the stock market and in lending money on mortgages. All this was a world away from the tradesman's upbringing which his father had known. Around the year 1910 his fortunes and those of his firm were at their height. He was Geographer to the King, his new premises in Long Acre were the centre of geographical publishing in England, his personal cash expenditure was around £4,000 per year, and his eldest son was being trained to follow him in the business as the third Edward Stanford. Strangely however, and although he could not possibly know it, the wheel had reached its highest point, and the greatest days were almost over.

BELOW: A typical page from Edward Stanford's private account books, for March 1888; it records a three-day holiday in Folkestone with his wife, Carrie: a new dress, cabs, trains, tips, telegrams, lunches and dinners.

Part Two **The Nineteenth Century World: A Portrait in Maps**

Stanford's international map publishing programme offers a rich and detailed picture of the Victorian world – of political changes, geographical exploration, colonial affairs and patterns of travel. All these maps were published for fundamentally the same reason: to satisfy public interest, and Stanford had to make a judgement whether that interest was ephemeral or long lasting, and how much to invest in satisfying it. A survey of the titles and dates of these maps invariably sheds light on the events and priorities of the time, and shows the way Stanford developed his business by responding to them. There is no doubt that Stanford was more strongly drawn to political mapping than to physical or scientific mapping. There was no counterpart in Stanford's output to the graphic presentation of physical geography which was typical of the new German school of cartography, and which strongly influenced Bartholomew. Instead Stanford filled his atlases with detailed maps showing the latest colonies, the theatres of war, the results of the latest treaties, and the latest railway and telegraph lines. This expertise was undoubtedly enriched by Stanford's private mapmaking activities for the War Office, the Colonial Office and the Foreign Office. It must also have helped Stanford to secure the contracts to produce such maps as those drawn for the great diplomatic reference books by Sir Edward Hertslet, *The Map of Europe by Treaty,* 1875-91, and *The Map of Africa by Treaty,* 1894. Hertslet, who was librarian and archivist at the Foreign Office, was a member of the British delegation to the Berlin Conference of 1878–79, where he must have come into frequent contact with John Bolton.

EUROPE

In Europe the end of the Napoleonic era was followed by four decades of peace, a peace ended by the Crimean War of 1853–55, in which Russia was opposed by Britain, France and Turkey. Beneath the immediate causes of this conflict (the rights of various religious groups in the Ottoman dominions and in the Holy Land) lay Britain's deep and continuing mistrust of Russia's political ambitions in Asia and Eastern Europe, a mistrust which led to a British policy of supporting Turkey as a bulwark against Russia. This suspicion of Russia was a fundamental component in British foreign policy throughout the mid- and late-nineteenth century, and it began to weaken only after 1880 with the rise of German power. It explains

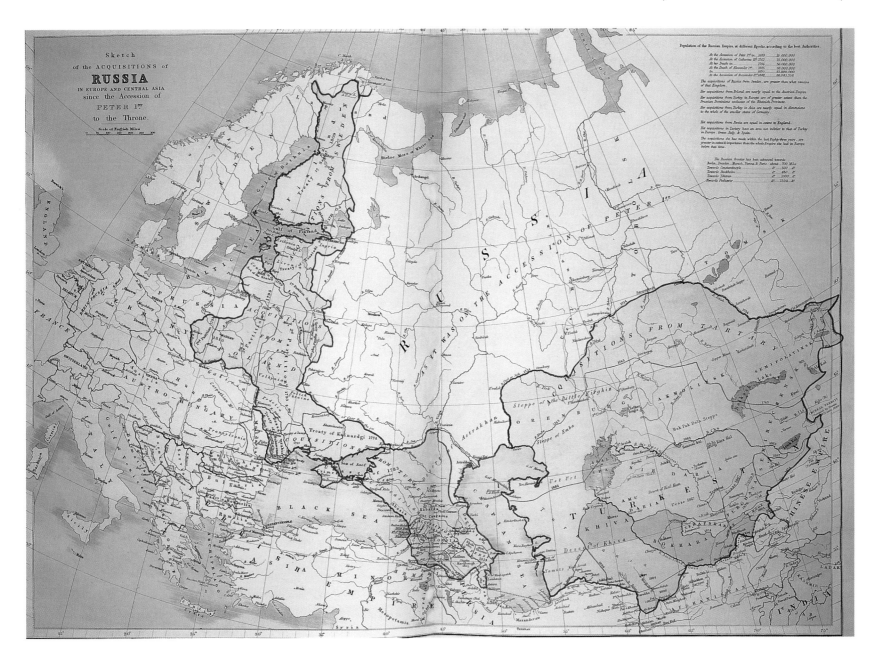

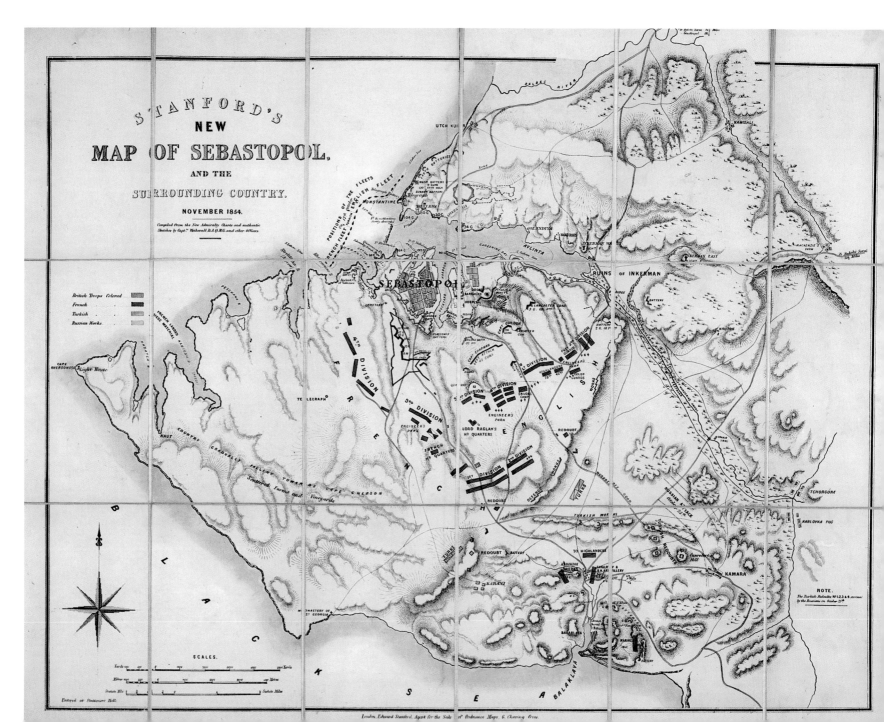

a rather curious map which Stanford published in the 1887 folio edition of the *London Atlas,* a map entitled *The Acquisitions of Russia since the Accession of Peter the Great.* This map shows the steady expansion of Russian territory over a century and half, southward and eastward from the original kingdom of Muscovy, with the clear implication that this process might be expected to continue. The map was originally drawn by John Arrowsmith, and was one of those taken over by Stanford when he bought Arrowsmith's copper-plates in 1874. It originated as an illustration to the book *The Progress and Present Position of Russia* by Sir John MacNeill, published by Murray in 1836, a polemical work warning against Russian expansionism. The fact that this map was revised and reprinted in 1887, and again in the 1893 edition of the *London Atlas,* shows how deep seated this feeling about Russia was. Significantly it was dropped from the third edition in 1904, by which time Britain and France were building their new friendship with Russia to counterbalance the German threat. In connection with the Crimean War itself, Stanford published a *General Map of Crimea and Adjacent Territory* in 1855, and two specific war maps, one of the Battle of Alma River, which took place on 20 September 1854, and another showing the disposition of the forces during the siege of Sevastopol, which lasted from October 1854 until September 1855. It was the Russian evacuation of Sevastopol which marked the effective end of hostilities.

War maps of this kind were of course ephemeral – none of these Crimea maps was being advertised in Stanford's 1858 catalogue – and Stanford set out to create permanent reference mapping of Europe in his *Library Map* of 1858, drawn at the very large scale of 1:3.2 million. This map presents a magnificent snapshot of mid-nineteenth century Europe, essentially unchanged since the Treaty of Vienna, and immediately before the momentous changes which created a new political landscape between 1859 and 1871. Historically the main focuses of interest lie in Italy and Germany, both still divided among their pre-unification kingdoms. The whole of Southern Italy was then under the rule of the Spanish Bourbons; in the North, Lombardy and Venetia were part of the Austrian Empire; while between them lay "The States of the Church". In the very month in which this map was being printed – June 1858 – Camillo Cavour, Prime Minister of Piedmont, was secretly planning with Napoleon III of France to provoke a war against Austria, out of which would grow an unstoppable movement towards Italian independence and unification, which was substantially achieved by spring 1861. As events were unfolding in Italy, Stanford published in 1859 a *Map of the Seat of War in Italy.* The lesson of Italy was not lost on the other side of the Alps, where Bismarck set out to forge a united Germany in which Prussia would dominate the old kingdoms of Bavaria, Wurttemberg, Saxony and the others which are shown here. To achieve this he had first to establish Prussia's pre-eminence over Austria in the German-speaking world, which he did in the course of a brief war in

ABOVE: **Italy and the Alps from the Stanford *Library Map of Europe*, 1858, showing the pre-unification states.**
The Bodleian Library

OPPOSITE: **The siege of Sebastopol in the Crimean War, in a detailed Stanford map of 1854.**
The U.K. Hydrographic Office

1866. Austria–Hungary still extended across central Europe, bordering the Ottoman territories, shown here simply as Turkey. The provinces within Turkey named here – Wallachia, Rumili, Moldavia and so on – were ruled by local Islamic potentates who paid lip service only to the Sultan in Constantinople, and who were often contending against nationalist movements; the Ottoman Empire was in a process of disintegration.

Beyond the question of political boundaries, this map shows a new social force at work: the spread of the railways. Britain, France and Germany are liberally crisscrossed with rail lines, but in Scandinavia even Stockholm and Christiania (Oslo) are not yet linked; Italy has no track south of Florence, but a line is in progress from Rome to Naples; in Spain, Madrid to Valencia and Madrid to Lisbon have been begun; in Hungary the tracks stop a hundred miles east of Budapest, while in Russia there is only the one line linking Moscow and St. Petersburg. Submarine telegraphs are beginning to be marked, but their progress through the Mediterranean was slow: Malta as an important British naval base was linked, but Alexandria in the pre-Suez Canal days, was not. Elegantly engraved by the elder Keith Johnston, this map was a magnificent reference source for libraries and travellers, but Stanford could surely never have envisaged how quickly it would be overtaken by political events and require major revision. The *Library Map of Europe* was justifiably praised by the reviewer in the *Athenaeum* as "a work of science as to drawing and correctness; a work of art as to clearness and beauty."

Poland was another country in Europe which shared aspirations towards independence, having been under Russian control since 1815. In January 1863 an insurrection of Polish patriots broke out which lasted until it was crushed in April 1864. There was considerable sympathy in Britain for the Poles, and Stanford reflected something of the public mood when he published in April 1863 a *Map of the Kingdom of Poland showing its Present and Past Extent and the Successive Seizures of its Territories by Russia, Austria and Prussia*.

Bismarck's opportunity to unite Germany came with the nationalist fervour of the Franco-Prussian War of 1870–71. Europe watched in amazement as the German army cut through France in a few weeks, and besieged Paris on 19 September 1870. By October Stanford had published two highly graphic maps of the war: a panoramic view looking north from Strasbourg towards Paris, and a plan of *The Fortifications of Paris*. The latter included a descriptive text panel, edited from military reference works, which gave details of the *enceinte* (the city walls) and of the sixteen massive detached forts, which together had been designed to make Paris impregnable. The inevitable surrender came in January 1871, and the enlarged and unified Germany revolutionised both the map and the power balance of Europe.

From 1870 until the First World War the most contentious region of Europe was the Balkans, with the problem of restructuring the former Ottoman territories there. In 1861 the principalities of Moldavia

LEFT: **Stanford's *Map of the Kingdom of Poland showing its Present and Past Extent and the Successive Seizures of its Territories by Russia, Austria and Prussia,* 1863**
The Bodleian Library

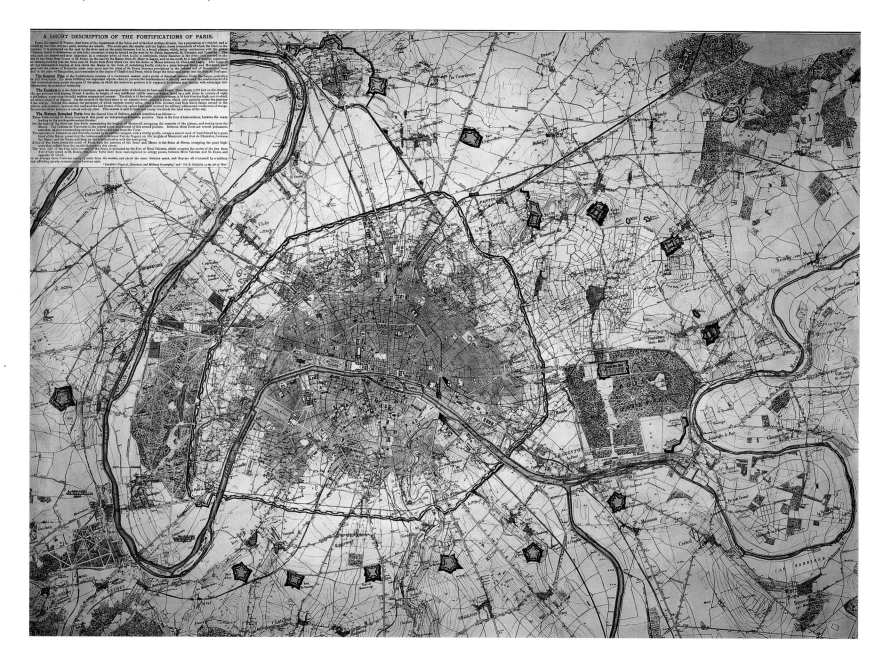

and Wallachia merged to form Romania. From 1874 onwards Bosnia, Herzegovina, Serbia and Montenegro all rebelled against Turkish rule, aided by Russian military intervention. Out of this war and the subsequent Congress of Berlin, orchestrated by Bismarck, emerged the new state of Bulgaria in the east, while the western states were to be under Austro-Hungarian administration, thus sowing the seeds of future disaster. The emergence of these nations was charted in Stanford's map of the Balkans, which included a textual panel giving a resume of the Berlin decisions. Stanford also supplied to the offices of state special maps to illustrate the complexities of Balkan politics, including one remarkable attempt to depict the races and religions of the region by colour shading. This Foreign Office map of 1897 carries the ominous note: "The areas inhabited by the various races cannot be separated by any distinct line of demarcation. They merge into one another." It might be thought that this region was of little direct concern to the people of Britain, Stanford's customers, but what did concern them constantly was the "balance of power" – that Russia or Austria or Germany might be acquiring influence or territory which could one day threaten Britain. One specific outcome of the Berlin Congress was the decision to place Cyprus under British administration, and this resulted in the first full topographic survey of the island, commissioned by the War Office and carried out by none other than the young Horatio Kitchener. A highly detailed map in sixteen sheets at a scale of one mile to the inch, it was engraved and published by Stanford, a remarkable example of an official surveying body using the expertise of a commercial partner. When this map appeared in 1882, *The Times* commented "One tangible and very valuable result of the English occupation of Cyprus has just appeared in the form of a very fine map published by Stanford … no more creditable production in cartography has ever been issued from any private establishment in this country." Stanford reduced this unique material to produce the best single sheet map of Cyprus then available, which formed part of the 1887 folio *London Atlas*.

Political change and conflict thus played a great part in Stanford's European map publishing, but of course tourism could not be neglected. Stanford naturally published maps of all the European countries and regions, but a number of them were in fact the Arrowsmith maps which he had acquired in 1874, and up dated where necessary, but which still looked slightly antiquated. Stanford was aware of this, and invested in drawing entirely new maps of those countries where the Arrowsmith maps had failed to do justice to the topography. The 1894 edition of the *Atlas* included a superb new map of Switzerland, with the mountain relief meticulously engraved, for which Stanford used the Swiss official survey maps as a model. In the 1904 edition a splendid two-sheet map of Italy in a similar style was included. Sadly we do not know the name of the engraver of these fine maps, but we do know that Stanford was sufficiently proud

OPPOSITE: **The fortifications of Paris shown in a Stanford map published during the Franco-Prussian War of 1870–71.**
The Bodleian Library

RIGHT: **The Balkans from the 1887** *London Atlas,* **with a text explaining the provisions of the Treaty of Berlin.**

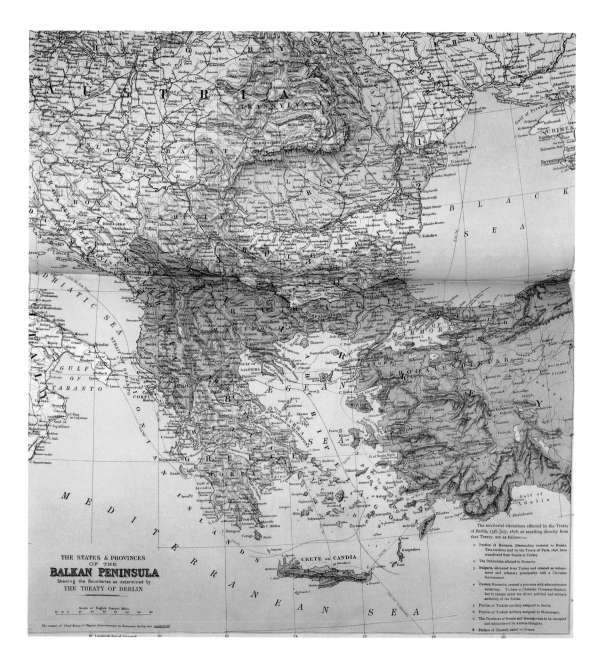

THE STATES & PROVINCES
OF THE
BALKAN PENINSULA
Shewing the Boundaries as determined by
THE TREATY OF BERLIN

Scale of English Statute Miles

The names of Chief Towns of Bulgaria (Governments) in European Turkey are underlined

The territorial alterations effected by the Treaty of Berlin, 13th July, 1878, or resulting directly from that Treaty, are as follows:—

1. Portion of Romania (Bessarabia) restored to Russia. This territory had by the Treaty of Paris, 1856, been transferred from Russia to Turkey.

2. The Dobrudsha allotted to Romania.

3. Bulgaria, alienated from Turkey and created an autonomous and tributary principality, with a Christian Government.

4. Eastern Roumelia, created a province with administrative autonomy. To have a Christian Governor-General, but to remain under the direct political and military authority of the Sultan.

5. Portion of Turkish territory assigned to Servia.

6. Portion of Turkish territory assigned to Montenegro.

7. The Provinces of Bosnia and Herzegovina to be occupied and administered by Austria-Hungary.

8. Portion of Thessaly ceded to Greece.

LEFT: **A special edition of the Balkans map, coloured for the Foreign Office in 1897 to show the complex ethnic geography of the region.**
The Public Record Office

of the Switzerland map that he printed a number copies of the physical relief plate only, with no place-names, so that the engraving might be admired as a work of art. But he made no secret of the fact that the cost of this kind of meticulous engraving was frightening, and that he could scarcely expect to profit from the map.

OPPOSITE: **Cyprus from the 1887 *London Atlas,* reduced from the highly detailed survey by Horatio Kitchener.**

AFRICA

In the maps of Africa which Stanford published between 1853 and 1914, two historical themes are dominant: the exploration of the great central region of the continent, and the colonial activities of the European nations. As early as 1853 Saunders and Stanford published a fine and detailed sketch map of *Africa from the Equator to the Southern Tropic,* which showed the routes and discoveries of the recent explorers. It was edited by William Desborough Cooley, one of the founders of the Hakluyt Society and an armchair expert on African geography. This map embodied the discoveries between 1848 and 1850 of Johann Rebmann and Johann Krapff, the first Europeans to see Mount Kilimanjaro and Mount Kenya. But the map's timing was unlucky, for the geography of that entire region was about to be revolutionised as European explorers attempted to unravel the enigmas of the great African rivers. Their motives were both intellectual and moral: to fill up the blank on the map – especially to answer the great question as to the source of the Nile – and to root out the slave trade and spread Christianity. Their hope was that the rivers would open up the interior of the continent to civilising influences, and bring about the defeat of the slavers. Between 1856 and 1863, Livingstone, Burton, Speke and Baker returned to England with their accounts of the Zambezi, and of the great lakes Victoria and Albert, which appeared to be perfectly located to fulfil the role of Nile source, although this had not been absolutely proved.

The first edition of Stanford's *Library Map of Africa,* 1866, is a fascinating transitional map, drawn and published while geographical knowledge was in the process of transformation. A large proportion of what appears on this map had in fact been unveiled only during the preceding fifty years: the trans-Saharan routes, the Ethiopian highlands and the Blue Nile, and the Zambezi region. The interest focuses now on the central region where the lakes appear, very imperfectly shown, while to the west of them is the huge void of the Congo basin, with a couple of phantom lakes outlined. The Nile is clearly given a dual source in Lakes Victoria and Albert, which are linked via the Ripon and Murchison Falls. If this map is compared with a later edition, published in 1890, the changes are huge: the Congo had been mapped by H.M. Stanley, along with the watershed dividing it from the Zambezi. Lake Edward and the Ruwenzori Mountains were the

OPPOSITE: **Central Africa from the 1887** *London Atlas*. **The English "sphere of influence" in the later Rhodesia, is squeezed between the many German territories and the older Portuguese colonies.**

trophies of Stanleys' final African adventure. The phantom lakes have vanished, but Lakes Rudolf, Moero and Bangweolo (the latter the place of Livingstone's death) have appeared. No less striking are the political changes as the shadow of European colonisation falls across the continent. The "possessions" of Britain, France, Germany, Portugal, Belgium and Italy are now colour coded. Another important process is only just beginning, however, that of replacing the tribal names which had always been used to identify the regions of Africa by the names of the new colonies. Ashanti has become the Gold Coast, but many more would follow in the next twenty years: Fulani and Hausa would become Nigeria, Matabele would become Rhodesia, and so on. The network of European communication, the railways and the telegraphs, is also being woven through and around Africa. The eastern marine telegraph runs from Suez around the Horn of Africa to Natal, and the western line runs from Gibraltar via the Guinea coast to Cape Town. In Egypt and the Cape Colony, the rail lines are well established, while the French had linked Tunis with Oran, and were laying track to Dakar. Stanford's advertisement for the first edition of this map is worth quoting in full:

"The geographical knowledge recently acquired on the great continent of Africa presents the most surprising examples of the rapid progress of modern science. The Great Sahara, formerly represented as a vast sandy waste, has been shown by a succession of noble explorers, from Denham and Clapperton to Duveyrier, to contain grand ranges of mountains, with varieties of scenery and other conditions very different from the terrible desert of our imagination. Further south, nearly the whole range of Soudan, from the Atlantic to the Red Sea, has been remodelled from the labours of the French in Senegal; of Barth, Baikie and others on the Niger; and of Von Heuglin, Petherick, Speke and Baker &c in the Upper Basin of the Nile. South of the Equator, vast spaces have been filled up by Livingstone, Burton, Speke and Grant, Du Chaillu and Anderson, while great improvements have been made by the Surveys of the Colonial Governments. Stanford's Library Map presents this accumulation of new discoveries for the first time in a general map on a large scale."

The race for African colonies and "spheres of influence" really gathered pace in the 1880s, fuelled by European power-politics. The principle, put crudely, was to secure treaties and grab land before your rival did. There may also have been in some quarters a genuine belief in Europe's civilising mission, especially in the anti-slavery movement. The slave trade across the Atlantic had been abolished, but slavery within Africa was still rife. These two motives, the imperial and the moral, are combined in a striking map drawn by Stanford for inclusion in the book *The Partition of Africa,* 1895, by J. Scott Keltie, secretary to the R.G.S. This

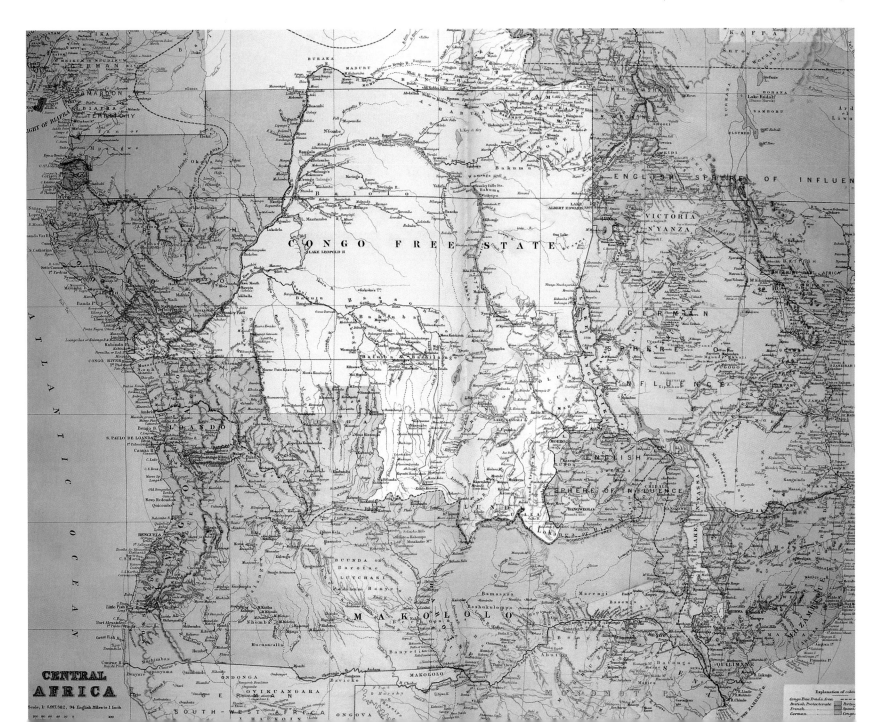

CENTRAL
AFRICA

Scale: 1: 5,977,382, 94 English Miles to 1 Inch

map illustrates both the general political situation, and some of the resolutions of the Brussels Conference of 1889-90, which discussed a strategy for bringing an end to the slave trade: roads and telegraphs were to be multiplied, military stations were to be staffed, and the importation of arms and liquor were to be severely restricted. It was ironic that such a conference should be hosted by Leopold II of Belgium, who was to become the most callous and mercenary of colonial overlords, presiding over unspeakable brutalities in his Congo territory.

As surveying activities were organised in the British colonies, so Stanford was able to publish the first detailed maps of them, maps such as that of the Gold Coast in six sheets at a scale of 1:253,440, 1902; of Southern Nigeria in ten sheets at 1:253,440, 1905; of the Nyasaland Highlands at 1:126,720, and of Zanzibar at 1:63,360, 1904. Rhodesia, being considerably larger, was published at 1:1 million scale in six sheets, as was British Somaliland. Some of these maps, the Southern Nigeria for example, were produced with the full cooperation of the War Office or the Colonial Office, who clearly found it convenient to use Stanford as a publishing partner. Others, like the Nyasaland map, were the work of civilian surveyors who would enter into a shared profit agreement with Stanford, similar to the commission publishing of books which was described in chapter one. It is not clear why Stanford did not publish maps of British East Africa – Uganda and Kenya. It is true that direct British involvement here developed rather later, but the Mombasa to Lake Victoria railway was completed by the British in 1903, and survey information was available; presumably the data acquired during the railway survey was not adequate to map the whole region. Stanford's cooperation with government departments was not restricted to maps of British colonies: when France occupied Tunis in 1881, the Foreign Office urgently needed to work out the implications for Britain, and commissioned from Stanford a map of the Mediterranean, centred on Tunis and giving distances to capital cities. This was fairly detailed, but still a sketch map, obviously intended as a working document which could be used in discussions and annotated as necessary. It is an interesting example of a privately commissioned map which Stanford could produce quickly, supplying perhaps a couple of hundred copies. It would not appear in any catalogue of Stanford's publications, nor be supplied to any other customers, but one copy happens to have survived in the Foreign Office archives.

British involvement in Egypt came about for a very clear-cut reason. When the Suez Canal was opened in 1869, the British suddenly awoke to its huge potential importance for India, and in 1875 bought out the shares in the canal owned by the bankrupt Khedive of Egypt. From the running of the Canal Britain progressed towards running Egypt, in spite of the fact that the country was nominally still a vassal of the Turkish Empire. From 1875 onwards a map of Egypt was an essential part of the Englishman's world atlas,

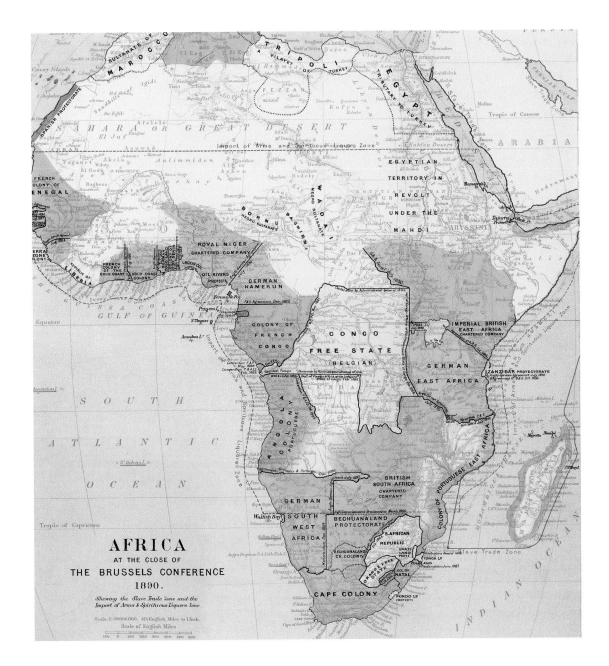

but Egypt here meant only the northern part, to perhaps one hundred miles south of Cairo, and there was no real reason to venture further into the inhospitable tropics of the Sudan. By 1881, however, a religious revolt was gathering from the south, and Britain found herself fighting it. British colonialism may have stemmed from the quest for economic rewards, but in the public mind it was sustained also by the legends built up around individuals – missionaries, explorers and soldiers, and none of these hero figures was more famous than General Gordon, whose life and death were responsible for Britain's pursuit of the Sudanese forces. From 1874 to 1880 Gordon served as governor of the province of Equatoria in the Sudan, during which time he mapped the upper reaches of the Nile. From Gordon's surveys a remarkable manuscript map was prepared by Stanford at a scale of 1:730,000, almost certainly drawn by John Bolton personally, and used as a basis for a number of later maps of the Upper Nile. After Gordon's death there was a huge public interest in books and souvenirs relating to him, and in 1885 Stanford published a facsimile of Gordon's own sketch map drawn in 1874 on his original journey from Suakin to Khartoum to take up his appointment as governor. The whereabouts of the original manuscript of this map is unknown. Both Edward Stanford and John Bolton had a special admiration for Gordon, and we know from Stanford's personal accounts that in May 1891 he spent eleven pounds on a fine bronze statuette of the dead hero, the work of the sculptor Hamo Thorneycroft, which he presented to his father.

The other great Africa personality whom Bolton knew well was H.M. Stanley, but there is something of a puzzle concerning their relationship. Bolton frequently met and corresponded with Stanley, and drew maps in 1878 relating to his Congo journey. Yet the maps which were published in Stanley's classic book *Through the Dark Continent,* 1878, were drawn not by Stanford, but by Edward Weller, a well-known freelance cartographer, who did a great deal of map work for John Murray and other publishers, and for the R.G.S. Whether the surviving Bolton-Stanley manuscripts were sketched for purely private interest or not, the fact remains that none of Stanley's books were illustrated by maps drawn by his friend Bolton.

The region of Africa in which Britain had the longest-standing, and ultimately the most costly interest, was of course South Africa. The Cape Colony was acquired by Britain from the Dutch during the Napoleonic wars, and before the building of the Suez Canal it was the midway port of call en route to India. Conflict between British settlers and the older Dutch inhabitants led to the Dutch trek northwards and the founding of the Orange Free State, Natal, and the Transvaal. The British annexed Natal in 1843, but the other two were left as Boer republics. Stanford published several fine maps of the Cape Colony which were unusual in showing the administrative districts with their distinctive English or Dutch names: Malmesbury, Worcester and Prince Albert, Swellendam, Oudtshoorn and Bredasdorp. The event which transformed the

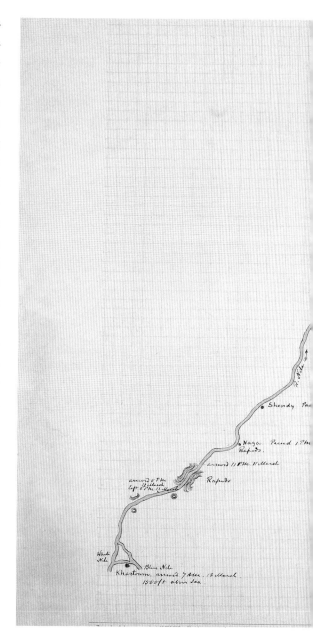

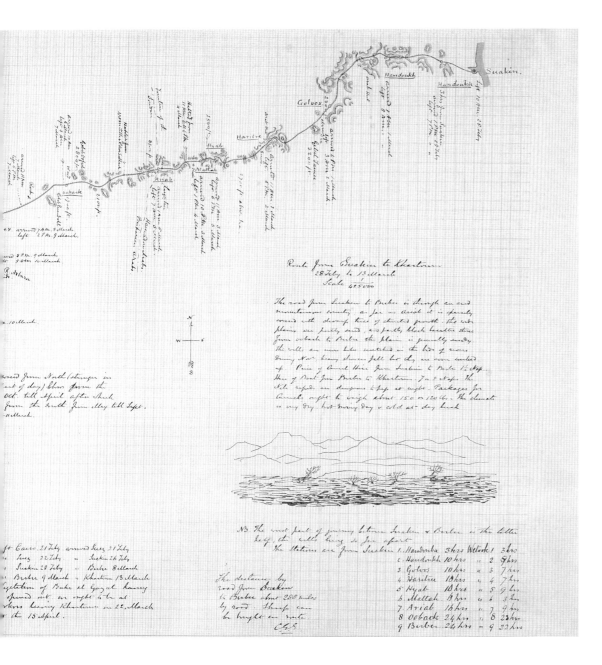

LEFT: **Facsimile published by Stanford in 1885 of a sketch map drawn by General Gordon to show his route from Suakin to Khartoum in 1874. This was one of the many Gordon souvenirs to be marketed after his death. The whereabouts of the original manuscript are unknown. It may have been in the personal possession of Edward Stanford or John Bolton.** The Bodleian Library

BELOW: **General Charles "Chinese" Gordon – imperial hero and Stanfords customer – fought in the Crimean War and in China during the Taiping Rebellion. In 1877 he was appointed Governor of Sudan, leaving in 1880. In 1884 he went back to relieve the garrison of Khartoum. Besieged by the Mahdi, his troops held out for 10 months. He died two days before relieving forces arrived.**

RIGHT: *Map of the White Nile* – a manuscript map probably drawn by John Bolton embodying the surveys made by General Gordon in 1875–76.
The Royal Geographical Society

RIGHT: **A souvenir map showing General Buller's relief of Ladysmith in the Boer War, published by Stanford in 1902.**
The Bodleian Library

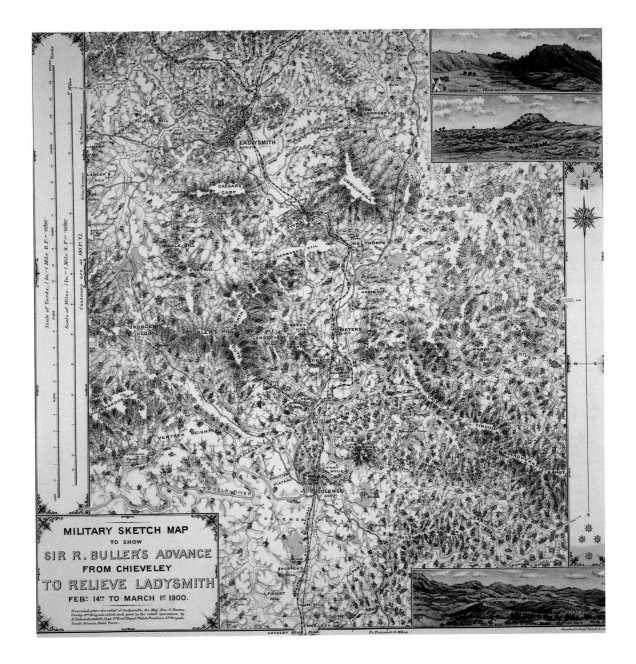

MILITARY SKETCH MAP
TO SHOW
SIR R. BULLER'S ADVANCE
FROM CHIEVELEY
TO RELIEVE LADYSMITH
FEB.Y 14TH TO MARCH 1ST 1900.

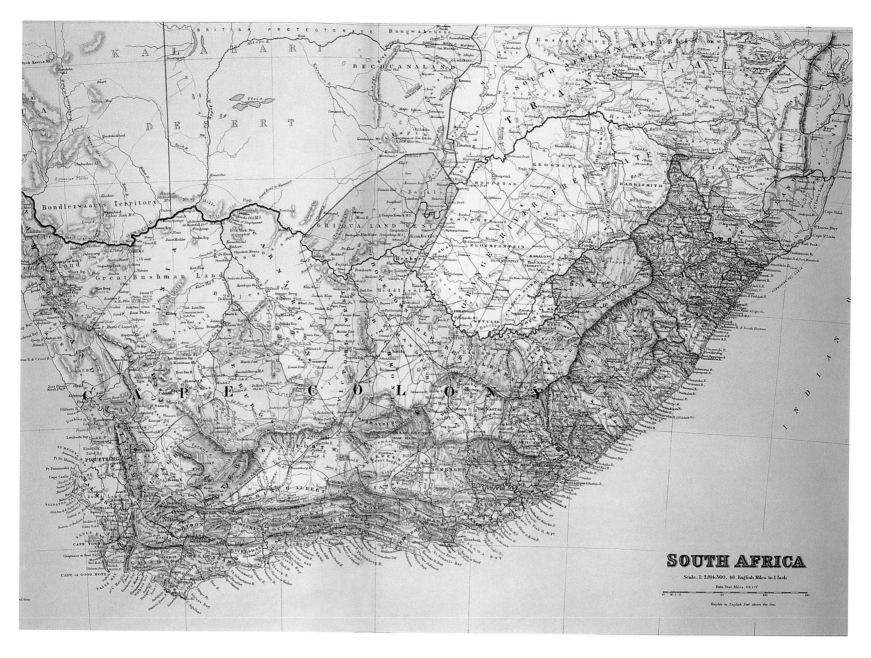

SOUTH AFRICA

Scale, 1: 2,814,560, 46 English Miles to 1 Inch

Brit. Stat. Miles. 69.1=1°

Heights in English Feet above the Sea.

course of South African history was the discovery of gold and diamonds in the Transvaal, attracting the British immigration into the Boer republics, and eventually leading to war between the two groups of Europeans. In the 1890s Stanford undertook the publication of several maps of the gold-bearing Transvaal, both topographic and geological. These increasingly detailed maps culminated in C.S. Goldman's *Atlas of the Witwatersrand Goldfields*, published as a commission work in 1899. This work comprised forty-two maps at the large scale of 1:14,880, in which thousands of numbered land parcels were shown. This project seems to have caused Stanford more headaches in drawing and printing than any other work that we know of. It tied up his draughtsmen and his presses for months, was the subject of endless difficulties and corrections, and lost him hundreds of pounds because he had underestimated its production costs. In the context of the Boer War itself Stanford published a number of special maps, including in 1902 an unusual two-part souvenir of the Relief of Ladysmith, in which a graphic relief map of the area was paired with a detailed sketch map showing the military positions during the British advance which lifted the siege.

The evolving image of Africa in nineteenth-century maps seems to symbolise something central in the mapmaker's imperial role: the assertion of control over territory. That control might be intellectual, as in the case of the explorer who dedicates himself to remove the blank on the map, or it might be political, as with the European statesman drawing boundary lines to define his "sphere of influence"; in either case, the European mastery of Africa had to be embodied in maps. At its crudest this resulted in the business office depicted in Forster's novel of 1910, *Howard's End,* where a map of Africa hung on the wall "looking like a whale marked out for blubber". But of course maps did serve more humane, civilising purposes too, and amid all the troubling reflections provoked by the colonial history of Africa, we should perhaps remember David Livingstone's words, when he wrote, "I view the end of the geographical feat as the beginning of the missionary enterprise."

ASIA

Unlike Africa, Asia was not virgin, conquerable territory. It had been for thousands of years the seat of ancient civilisations and religions, although it was precisely their decay in modern times that had offered possible lines of expansion to the European powers. Stanford's *Library Map of Asia,* first published in 1862 shows the continent divided between four empires: the Chinese, the Russian, and the Turkish, while the fourth was British India. In central Asia where these four powers approached or overlapped each other, there is an array of exotic regional names which evoke the history of Asia, but whose political status was obscure:

OPPOSITE: **South Africa from the 1887 *London Atlas,* showing the distinctive administrative place names, English and Dutch.**

OPPOSITE: **Kabul and the surrounding territory, 1880, drawn by Trelawney Saunders at the time of the Second Afghan War. The red lines show the British advance towards the city, while the blue line commemorates the disastrous British retreat of 1842.**
The Bodleian Library

Turkestan, the Great Horde, the Kirgis Steppe, Country of the Don Cossacks, the Tartar Khanate, and so on. There were perhaps four great political facts about Asia which currently concerned the British and which were therefore reflected in Stanford's mapping between 1853 and 1910. These were the expansion of Russia; the British presence in India; the decline of the Chinese Empire; and the location of the Holy Land within the senescent Ottoman Empire.

The first of these has been discussed already: since the reign of Peter the Great the Russians had been steadily extending their control eastwards and southwards, reaching the Pacific coast and founding the city of Vladivostok in 1861 (not shown on Stanford's *Library Map of Asia* incidentally), and the borders of Persia and Afghanistan, taking ancient cities such as Tashkent and Samarkand. These events were seen as a dark shadow gradually lengthening over the map of Asia and moving in the direction of British India. In 1840 Palmerston prophesied that "sooner or later the Cossack and the Sepoy, the man from the Baltic and the man from British India, must meet in central Asia". The only response to this threat was, as the British saw it, a "forward policy", a policy of pushing out from India itself and ringing it with buffer states to the north. The focus of tension was Afghanistan, and the Afghans' decision to receive a Russian mission at Kabul and refuse a British one led directly to the Second Afghan War of 1879. Stanford published two topical maps of Afghanistan in connection with this war, one a sketch map drawn by Trelawney Saunders showing the route of General Roberts's advance on Kabul, and the other showing the newly drawn frontiers following the Treaty of Gandamak, which was supposed to settle the dispute, although the later murder of a British envoy led to the British reoccupying Kabul. On the sketch map Saunders also marked the earlier event in Afghan history which had seared itself into the English memory – the 1842 evacuation of Kabul and subsequent massacre of thousands of British soldiers and civilians. Saunders' work in 1879 also resulted in a series of maps in the *Proceedings of the Royal Geographical Society*, illustrating a number of articles on Afghanistan.

In 1892, however, the Russians turned their gaze away from northern India towards the Far East, and began to build the trans-Siberian railway. Its completion in 1903 was marked by the publication of a Stanford map of the rail line, subtitled *The great land route to China and Korea*. If Russia had ambitions to annex territory from the effete Chinese Empire, she was bitterly disappointed, for she met instead humiliating defeat at the hands of Japan in the Manchurian War of 1904, again the subject of a topical "theatre of war" map from Stanford. The "Great Game" between Russia and Britain formed the subject-matter of a number of Stanford maps of Central Asia. One was commissioned by the publisher Archibald Constable in 1893 to illustrate a virulently anti-Russian book *The Rival Powers in Central Asia,* written by a

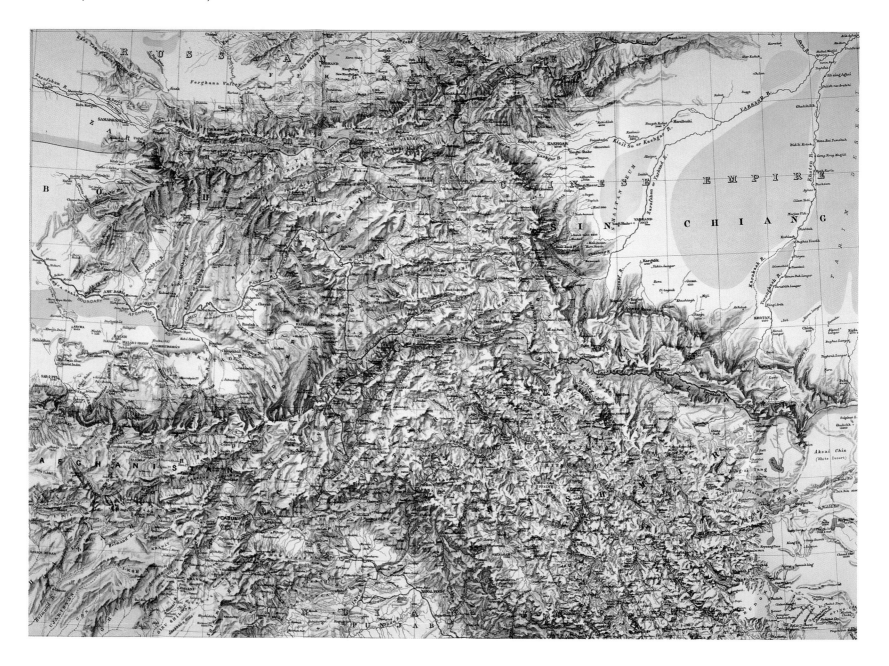

Polish patriot Josef Popowski. This map, showing the volatile region where the agreed boundaries between Russia, Britain and China faded into uncertainty in the wilderness of the Pamir Mountains, was subsequently included in the second and third editions of Stanford's folio *London Atlas.*

In 1857 India itself was the subject of the first large detailed wall map which Stanford ever published, a two-sheet map at a scale of 1:3 million. It was based on surveys made by the East India Company and by the Surveyor General of India, and showed the latest acquisitions of British India, including the province of Oudh which had been annexed in the previous year. The first rail lines in India are shown running north from Bombay and west from Calcutta, with many more sanctioned, such as those from Madras to Bombay and from Calcutta to Delhi. A chronological panel outside the map gives the history of the growth of British territories, beginning with the royal dowry of 1661 which included Bombay. Although this map was entitled *Stanford's Library Map of India* it was not uniform with the continental series: it was not drawn by Keith Johnston nor was it printed in-house by Stanford himself. The lettering and relief shading are noticeably different from, and inferior to, the later Johnston maps, and it is possible that this title was produced as a trial run for the others. 1857 was of course the year of the Indian Mutiny, and Stanford hastily issued a small topical map of *The Revolted Districts of British India,* which was really just an extract from this larger map showing a radius of 500 miles around Delhi where the drama of the Mutiny was enacted.

Two further significant maps of India's northern frontier lands deserve mention. One was an important example of Stanford's private cartographic activity for a government department: a map of the Himalayan region and published for the India Office in 1897, which showed the routes of explorers in those countries. Some of these explorers were westerners such as the famous Russian Prejevalsky, but the map also includes the routes of the native spies, known only by their initials, who were commissioned by the Survey of India to observe and survey the territories of these forbidding neighbours. This map was drawn to illustrate *A Memoir on the Indian Surveys 1875–1890* by Charles Black, an official account of the work of the Survey giving a great deal of information on the exploration of the Himalayas. The other map was of part of Nepal, Sikkim and southern Tibet, published commercially in 1904 to catch the public interest in the Younghusband expedition to Lhasa, undertaken to enforce trade and communication between India and the isolated land of Tibet. This map really concentrated on the route taken by Younghusband from Darjeeling to Lhasa through the Chumbi Valley on the border of Bhutan.

Ceylon (Sri Lanka) was never part of British India in the governmental sense, being administered by the Colonial Office and not by the India Office. Ceylon maintained its own official survey department, from which Stanford was able to obtain topographical material to construct a superlative eight-sheet map

OPPOSITE: **The North-West Frontier of India, 1893, drawn by Stanford to illustrate a political book, and included in the second edition of the London Atlas in 1893.**

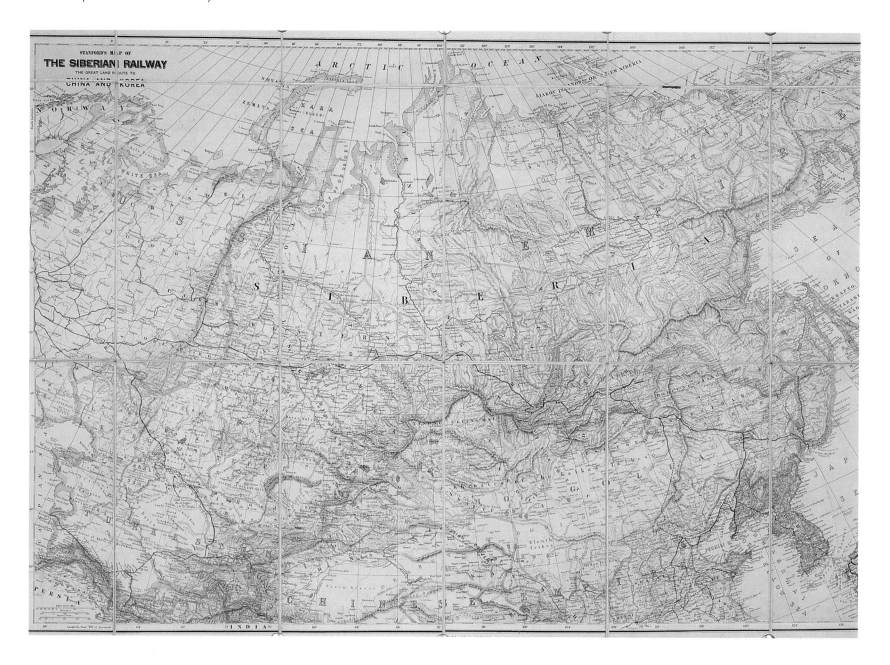

OPPOSITE: **Stanford's map of the newly opened Trans-Siberian Railway, 1893.**
The British Library

RIGHT: **Stanford's *Library Map of India,* 1857, a large, superbly detailed map published in the year of the Mutiny.**
The Hydrographic Office

OVER PAGE: **Stanford's map of the telegraph lines to India, drawn for the India Office by Trelawney Saunders, no date, but around 1880.**
The British Library

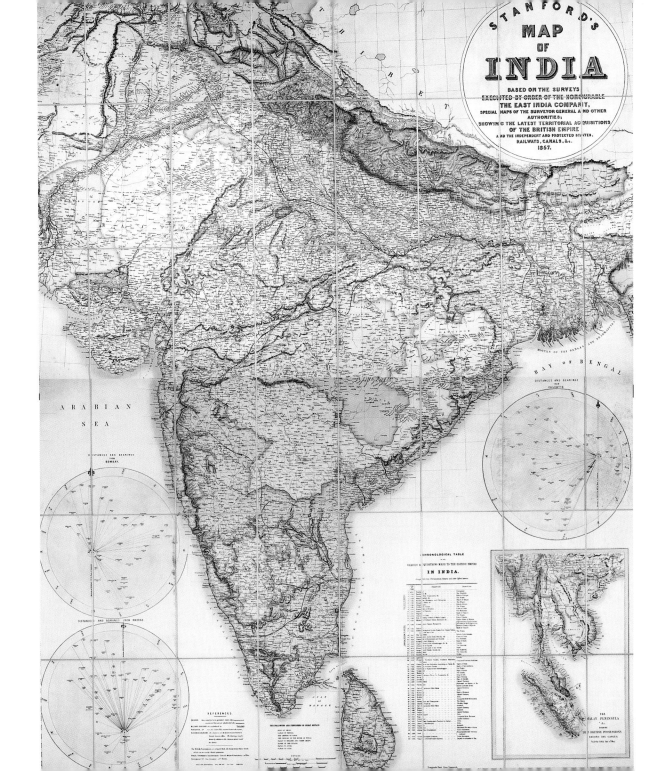

of the island at a scale of 1:253,440. This was edited and reduced to give an excellent, smaller scale map for the *London Atlas* series.

The case of China was unusual in terms of mapping. Politically and militarily senile, China became the object of European attention from the 1830s onwards. Various conflicts were engineered by the Russians, the French and the British, which resulted in enforced diplomatic agreements, the establishment of trading stations such as Hong Kong and Shanghai, and the freedom to begin missionary activity. With the exception of the missions, the British presence was always restricted to the treaty ports, and modern survey information of the country was unavailable. This explains why there could be no question of any initiative to map China, and why only general atlas maps of the country at scales of around 1:5 million were published, copied from whatever sources the commercial map publisher could lay his hands on. In 1911 Stanford published a somewhat more detailed map at a scale of 1:3 million for the China Inland Mission, claimed to have been prepared with the cooperation of the Chinese Imperial Post Office. If customers complained, as they did occasionally, about small-scale general maps such as these, Stanford or Bolton would reply that they "could not make bricks without straw": if no topographic surveys were carried out by foreign governments or by colonial powers, the public could not be provided with authentic maps. As late as 1900, maps of Burma and Indo-China were rather sketchy, showing only the coasts and the main rivers, while the interior of the countries remained practically unmapped. Very different was the smaller and commercially more important region of Malaya, with its tin and rubber. Singapore and the individual districts – Pahang, Perak, and Negri Sembilan – which made up the Federated Malay States, were all the subject of highly detailed Stanford maps, while the whole peninsula was covered in a very fine map in six sheets at a scale of 1:506,880, all drawn from up to date topographic surveys.

At the other extremity of Asia there existed historical and religious motives for mapmaking. The revival of evangelical religion in the early nineteenth century greatly stimulated interest in the Holy Land – in making it accessible to Christian scholars and pilgrims. The British rapprochement with Turkey offered an opportunity to break down the long isolation of Palestine from the Christian west. Like most other map publishers, Stanford published numerous educational maps of the Holy Land, illustrating Old Testament and New Testament history, and special topics such as the journeys of St. Paul. These maps were designed by scholars from bodies such as the Society for the Promotion of Christian Knowledge, and simplified editions aimed at Sunday schools were also published. Stanford was in a strong position to issue high quality maps of this kind because in 1880 he had cooperated in publishing the most detailed modern topographic map of Palestine produced to that date. This was the *Map of Western Palestine prepared from surveys conducted for the*

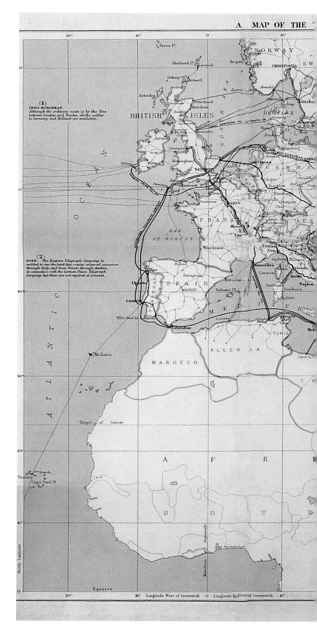

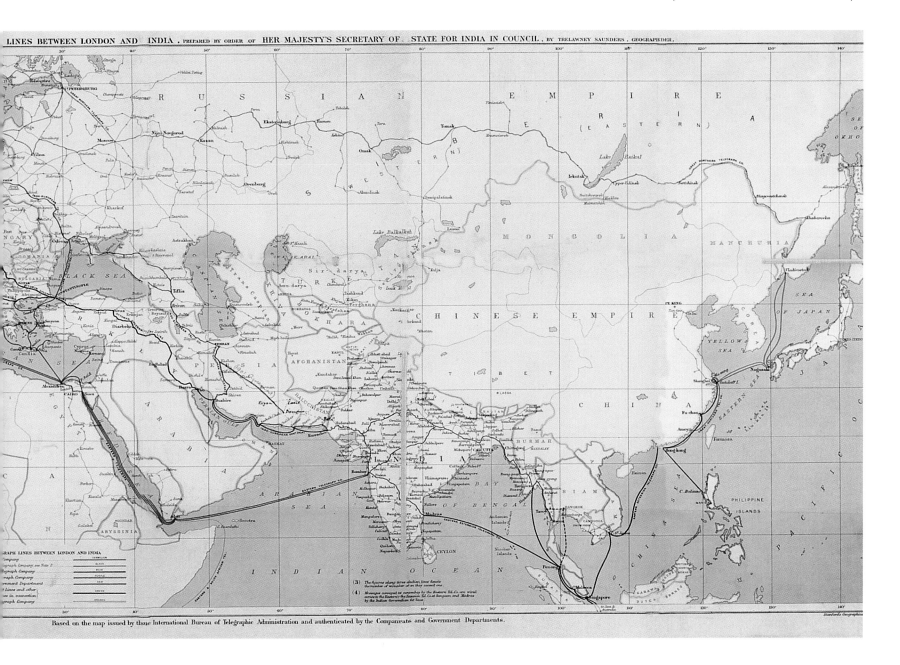

LINES BETWEEN LONDON AND INDIA. PREPARED BY ORDER OF HER MAJESTY'S SECRETARY OF STATE FOR INDIA IN COUNCIL, BY TRELAWNEY SAUNDERS, GEOGRAPHEDER.

Based on the map issued by the International Bureau of Telegraphic Administration and authenticated by the Companeats and Government Departments.

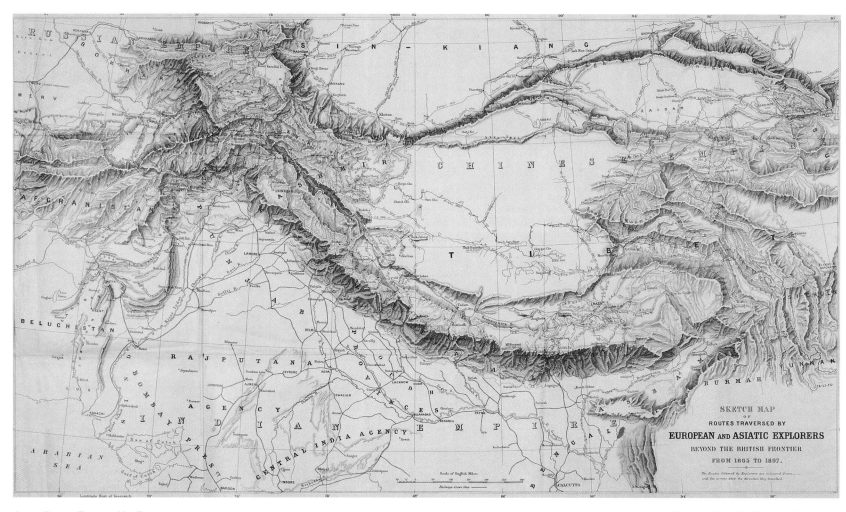

ABOVE: *Routes Traversed by European and Asiatic Explorers Beyond the Indian Frontiers,* c.1898, published for the India Office to accompany a book on the work of the Survey of India.
The British Library

OPPOSITE: **Stanford's map of the route of the Younghusband expedition to Tibet, 1904.**
The British Library

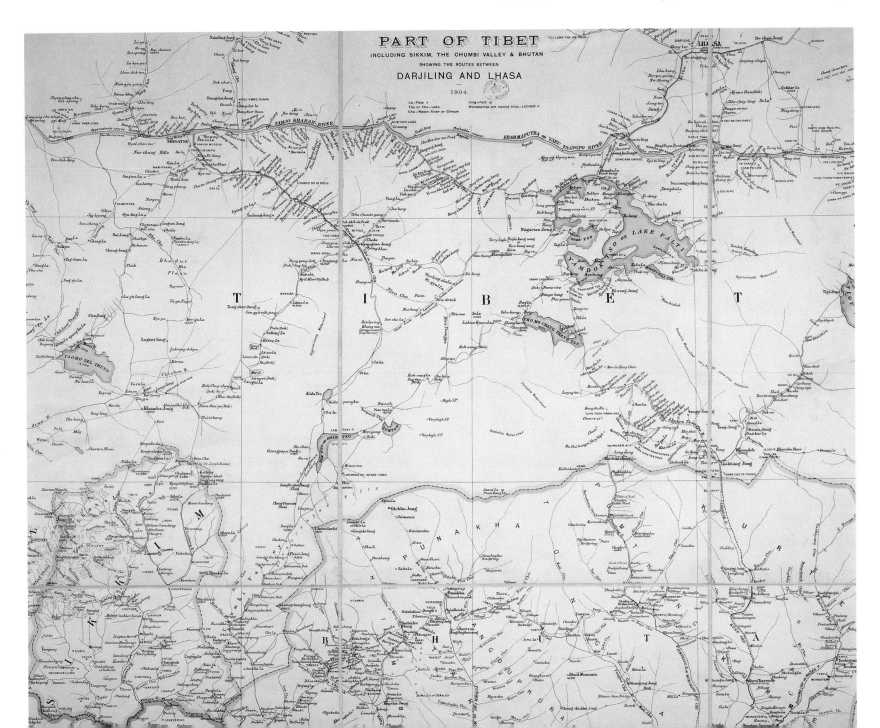

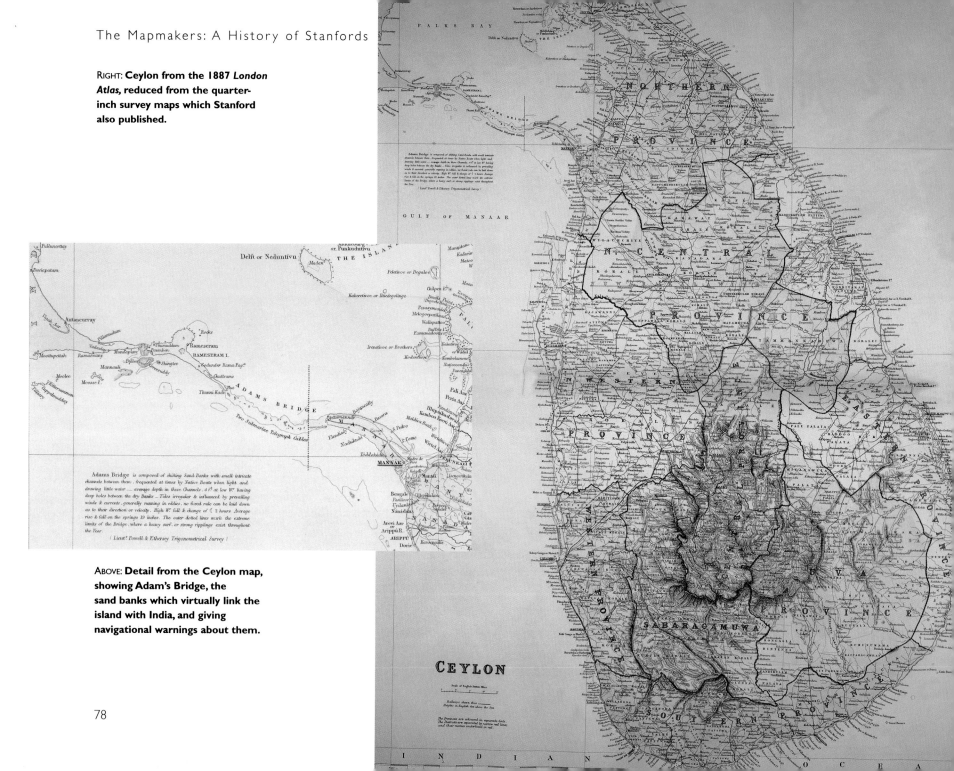

RIGHT: **Ceylon from the 1887** *London Atlas,* **reduced from the quarter-inch survey maps which Stanford also published.**

ABOVE: **Detail from the Ceylon map, showing Adam's Bridge, the sand banks which virtually link the island with India, and giving navigational warnings about them.**

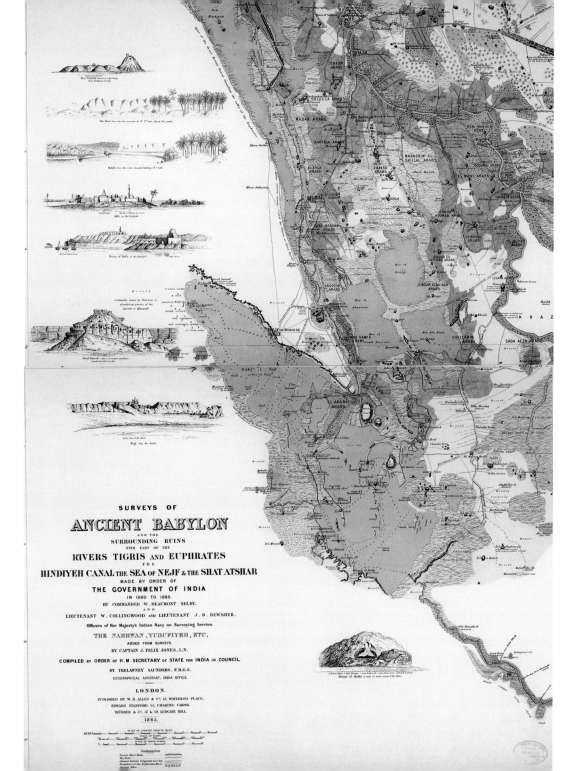

LEFT: **A section from *Surveys of Ancient Babylon,* a superbly detailed and artistic map published by Stanford in 1885.**
The U.K. Hydrographic Office

OPPOSITE: **Arabia drawn by Trelawney Saunders to illustrate the book *The Annals of the Early Caliphate*, 1883, by Sir William Muir.**
The British Library

BELOW: **The region around Troy, drawn by Stanford to illustrate the English edition of Schliemann's *Troja*, published by John Murray in 1883.**
The Bodleian Library

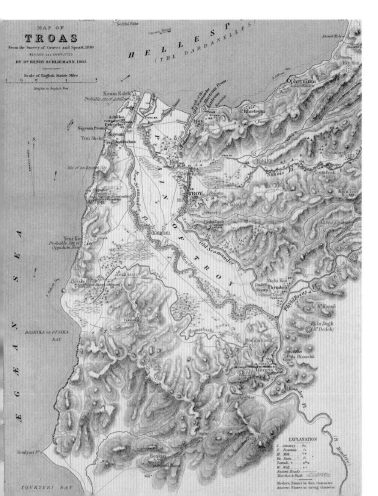

Committee of the Palestine Exploration Fund by Lieutenants Kitchener and Conder of the Royal Engineers. It was drawn at a scale of one inch to one mile and occupied twenty-six sheets. The facilities of the Ordnance Survey were used to make the printing plates, and Stanford carried out the printing. Stanford's publicity claimed that the level of detail on this map would probably never be surpassed, and the list of features included certainly seemed to justify this claim: "Vineyards, orchards, gardens, woods, shrub, palms, fir-trees, marsh, sand, perennial streams, dry watercourses, wells, pools, aqueducts, springs, cisterns, bridges, tombs, sarcophagi, caves, mosques, churches, survey camps, ruins, wine-presses, watch-towers, Roman mile-stones, electric telegraphs, roads, tracks, trigonometrical stations, bench-marks, altitudes above sea-level and depressions below the same." This map was destined to be reprinted by the British military authorities in 1916 when detailed topographical maps were required for the campaigns in this region.

Christianity was not the only subject of historical interest in the Near East. Trelawney Saunders drew a fine Stanford map of the Arabian peninsula to illustrate the life of Mahomet, published in the book *Annals of the Early Caliphate,* 1883, by Sir William Muir, the distinguished oriental scholar. In his preface to this book Muir warmly acknowledged Saunders's help and expertise. Saunders was at work again as draughtsman and editor of an unusual large and picturesque map of *Ancient Babylon and its Surrounding Ruins.* Published in 1882, this work was based on surveys carried out between 1860 and 1865 by officers of the Survey of India, and it was produced by order of the Secretary of State for India. The context of this survey was the enlightened rule in Baghdad in the 1860s of Midhat Pasha, who modernised and reformed many aspects of life in Ottoman-ruled Iraq, and who cultivated diplomatic relations with the western powers, permitting visits by archaeologists and scholars to the region of ancient Mesopotamia. Yet another area of western Asia which was of intense interest to European scholars was the site of the legendary city of Troy, in north-west Asia Minor. It was Stanford who was commissioned to draw the map illustrating Heinrich Schliemann's historic book *Troja,* when it appeared in the English edition by John Murray in 1883. This area was judged to be of sufficient interest to include a large-scale map of "Dardanelles and the Troad" in the folio *London Atlas* of 1887, but of course Stanford little realised how significant the names Dardanelles and Gallipolli would become a generation later in 1915.

The European view of Asia in the late nineteenth century was perfectly summed up in the preface to the *Asia* volume in Stanford's *Compendium,* contributed by Sir Richard Temple, politician and former Indian administrator. Temple paid tribute to Asia's role as the cradle of civilisation, and dwelt on the importance of its ancient sites, the magnificence of its geography and of its flora and fauna. Yet he judged its religions to be crude and irrational, and to have withered the minds and energies of its peoples. He contrasted China, lacking in wealth, education, justice and railways, with India, now enriched materially and morally by the British presence. A third of the population of Asia was now under the dominion of European

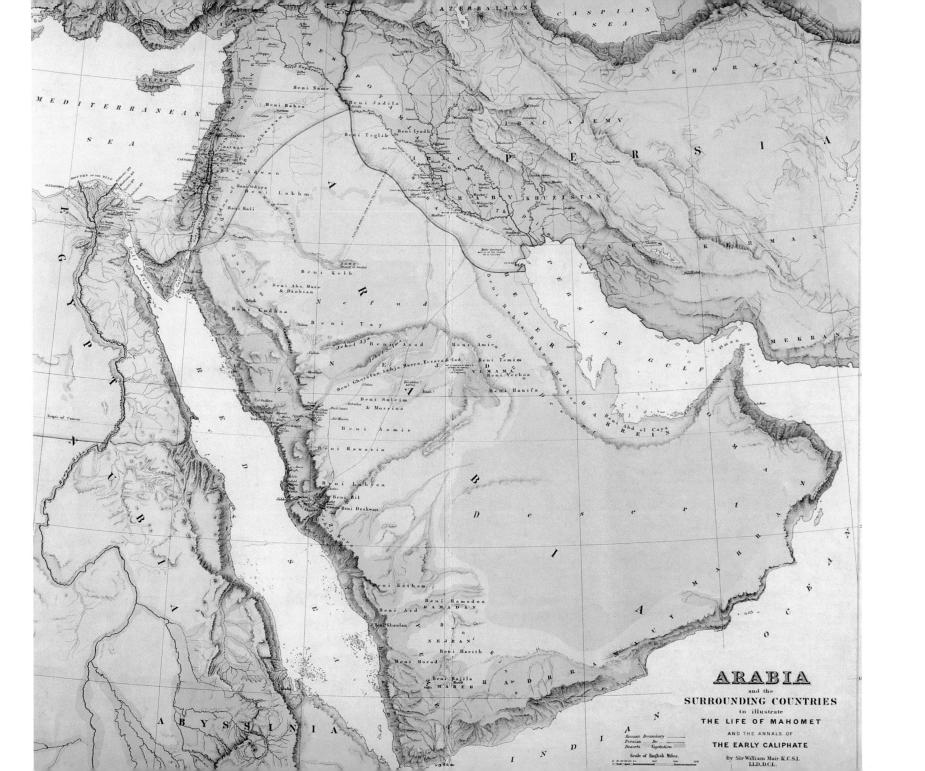

ARABIA
and the
SURROUNDING COUNTRIES
to illustrate
THE LIFE OF MAHOMET
AND THE ANNALS OF
THE EARLY CALIPHATE

By Sir William Muir K.C.S.I.
LL.D.,D.C.L.

Roman Boundary
Persian   Do
Deserts   Vegetation

Scale of English Miles.

RIGHT: **Stanford's *Library Map of North America,* 1863. The original is almost two metres across, and has been dissected and mounted on cloth for folding into a leather library case. Alaska (see page 84) is named as "Russian America", and Greenland (see detail opposite) as "Danish America".**
The U.K. Hydrographic Office

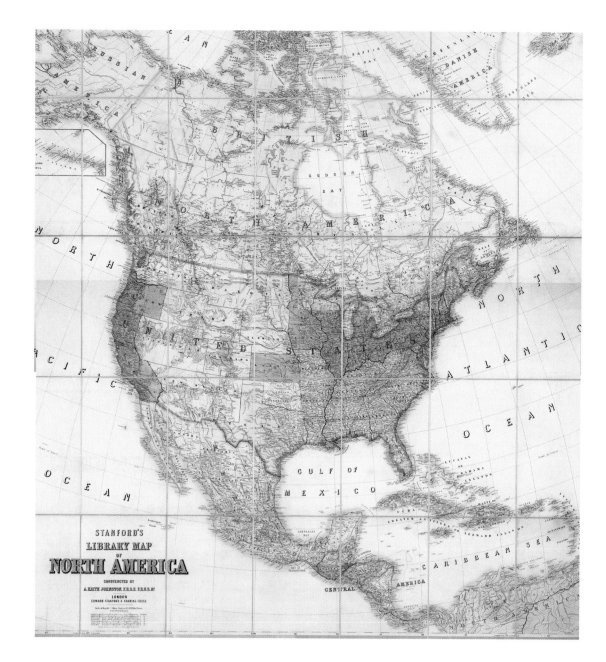

powers, and history had clearly decreed that it was Asia's destiny to be guided and led into a new era by European influences. In this view, the European colonies in Asia, and elsewhere too presumably, were the agents of an inevitable Darwinian process of social evolution, while most aspects of these ancient cultures were considered to be doomed to extinction.

THE AMERICAS

It was in 1845 that an American journalist declared, "It is our manifest destiny to overspread the continent allotted by Providence for the free development of our yearly multiplying millions." In the year 1800 the United States occupied an area of around 800,000 square miles lying entirely east of the Mississippi. By 1900 it had expanded to more than three million square miles, spread across the entire continent to the Pacific Ocean. While imperial ambitions had driven Britain, France, Germany and Russia to range through Asia and Africa, the United States had found a built-in empire awaiting its people at home. When Stanford commenced publishing his maps of the United States in the early 1860s the era of exploration was all but over, for pioneers such as John Fremont had traversed and mapped much of the mountain region looking for routes which settlers could follow to the western coastal states. Army engineers had been busy surveying the Mexican border region of the south–west, while a further motive was the plan to build railroads from the east to the Pacific coast. Oregon had been acquired from the British by negotiation in 1846, California from the Mexicans by war in 1848, and both territories achieved statehood in the following decade. Both regions were rich in natural resources, including gold, and were a magnet to thousands from the east wishing to migrate.

Lying between east and west were vast territories of prairie and mountain, which were not them-selves the target of the early settlers. These territories – Utah, Nebraska, Kansas, Washington, New Mexico – had been annexed or purchased by the United States, but were not yet under organised government, and in some cases had white populations of only a few thousand. The Stanford maps of the following fifty years would chart the way these territories were subdivided and achieved statehood. The map publisher had to monitor these political events carefully, and keep his maps current. Within months of printing the first copies of the *Library Map of North America* in the summer of 1863, Stanford had to revise the plate in order to show the new territory of Arizona, which had been carved out of the former territory of New Mexico. Again, in 1892, Stanford's American agent had reason to write and complain that the current edition of that map pre-dated the division of North and South Dakota, to which Stanford could only reply that it would be

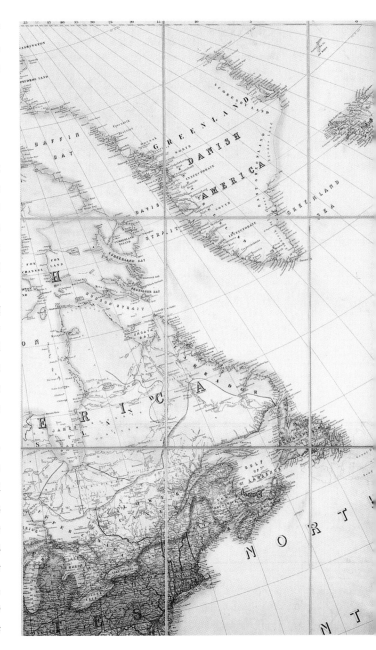

corrected at the next printing. The first edition of the *Library Map* of 1863 shows some splendid traces of early American history, such as Alaska named as "Russian America", and Greenland as "Danish America". Indian tribal names such as Navajo, Shoshone and Blackfoot fill the western half of the map, while in the east railways are everywhere, from the eastern seaboard to Chicago and then south to Mississippi and the Carolinas. In the 1880s, when the trans-continental rail lines to the Pacific had been completed, Stanford published a *Railway Map of the United States and Part of Canada*, but this was not simply aimed at the traveller, for the map's subtitle claimed to show clearly all the railway companies quoted in the daily Stock Exchange lists – testimony to the level of international investment in the worldwide rail industry.

The first edition of the *Library Map* pre-dated by four years the union of Upper and Lower Canada (Ontario and Quebec), and the only other Canadian territory named is British Columbia, designated a colony in 1858 when gold was discovered in the Fraser River. The region draining into Hudson's Bay still bears its historic name "Rupert's Land", the name originally bestowed on it in the Hudson's Bay Company charter of 1670, named for Prince Rupert, a cousin of King Charles II and the Company's first governor. The Yukon Territory likewise acquired its own identity with the gold-rush of 1897. A Stanford Yukon map was quickly produced in that year, showing the dense cluster of names that had sprung up around Dawson City, with every rivulet flowing into the Klondike given such hopeful names as "Bonanza Creek" or "El Dorado Creek". The gold discovery in the Klondike brought to a head the long-standing dispute between Canada and the United States concerning the eastern boundary of the Alaska panhandle, and Stanford produced an altered edition of his Yukon map showing the rival claims. In 1903 an international tribunal divided the disputed territory, giving a decision which marginally favoured the United States. Earlier the exploration and mapping of British Columbia had been advanced in the 1850s by the reconnaissance of John Palliser, commissioned by the Hudson's Bay Company to survey the region. Palliser's journals and reports were printed and presented to Parliament in May 1863, with sketch maps drawn by Stanford to show natural resources, and a magnificent *General Map of the Routes in British North America Explored by the Expeditions under Captain Palliser.* This map was actually commissioned by the Colonial Office from John Arrowsmith, but after Arrowsmith had spent a claimed two thousand hours research and drafting, the Colonial Office lost patience with him, and asked Stanford to take over the work. Even so the map was not finally completed until 1865. It stretched from Lake Superior to Vancouver, and was the finest map of western Canada produced in its time, by virtue of its topographical detail and its extensive notes on routes and natural resources. Palliser's surveys were a significant factor in encouraging British development of British Columbia. In Canada enormous interest centred on the mapping of the Arctic regions, for the

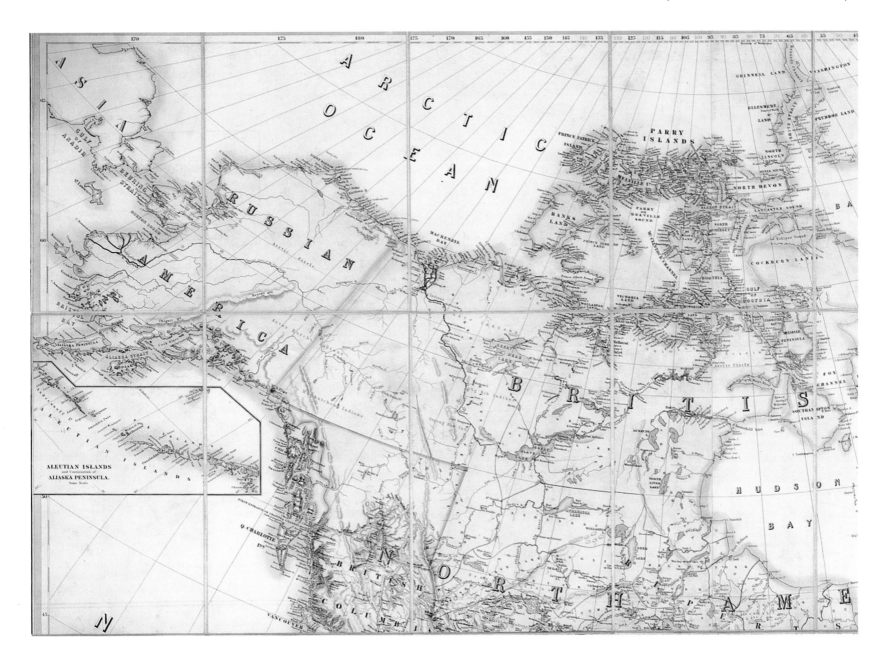

RIGHT: **The Yukon District, published
after the gold-rush of 1897 and
included in the third edition of the
London Atlas, 1904.**
The U.K. Hydrographic Office

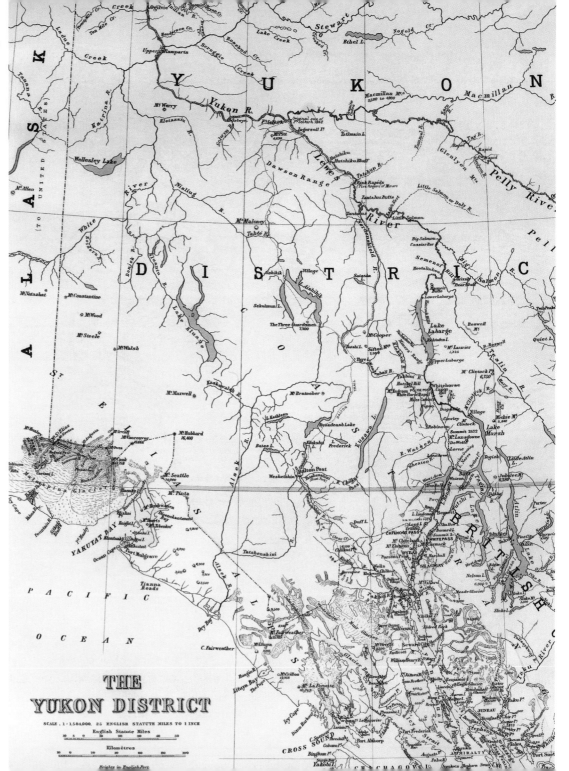

North-West Passage was still inviolate, and memories of the Franklin tragedy were still fresh: on the *Library Map* a note near King William Land marks the spot where his ships *Erebus* and *Terror* were abandoned in April 1848, although ten years were to pass before the expedition's terrible fate became known. Arctic exploration from the era of Davis and Frobisher to that of Greeley and Peary was the subject of a special map in the folio *London Atlas,* which was continually up-dated through many editions. The early editions printed the words "Unexplored Polar Regions" across the Pole itself, before it was known that this was an ice-cap and not a land mass.

Stanford's mapping activities in connection with the Americas had commenced as early as 1852, when Trelawney Saunders drew a series of three maps to illustrate *A Journal of a Trip to Darien* by Lionel Gisborne, an engineer whose purpose was to survey a possible route for a canal linking the Atlantic and Pacific Oceans. The position shown on these maps is around 100 miles east of where the Panama Canal would eventually be built. This material was later incorporated into a general map of Central America at 1:2 million scale that was first published in 1856 and which Stanford kept in his catalogue for over fifty years. A topical map with a shorter life was the map of the United States which Stanford published in March 1861 showing the seven states which had then seceded from the Union, and giving statistics of their free and slave populations. In the following month a plan of the harbour and forts at Charleston was issued, showing the scene of the Confederate attack on Fort Sumter which opened the Civil War. The base used for the Civil War map was simply a version of Stanford's "Hand-Map" of the United States, one of a series of small-scale reference maps which Stanford developed in the 1860s. Another copy of this same base map has been preserved in the Foreign Office archive, extensively annotated by Edward Hertslet, the diplomatic historian, to show the way the United States – Canada border had been gradually defined from the ending of the war of 1812 until 1874. Hertslet never published a volume on American maps and treaties to match his works on Europe and Africa, but this map shows that he was assembling the relevant materials.

British involvement in the Caribbean had a very long history, but by 1850 this region had lost some its old commercial importance following changes in the market for sugar and the abolition of slavery. Nevertheless the British presence provided the material for some high quality survey maps, such as the 1888 map of Jamaica at 1:174,240, the twelve-sheet map of Trinidad from 1899, or the plan of Belize City at 1:1080 in fourteen sheets – the latter an extraordinary map, with some sheets showing nothing but the jungle which reached the city's edge with hundreds and hundreds of trees individually drawn. These maps were drawn and printed by Stanford from survey data supplied from source by the offices of the Surveyors-General, and Stanford would then handle the commercial sales outside the colony itself. Change was slow

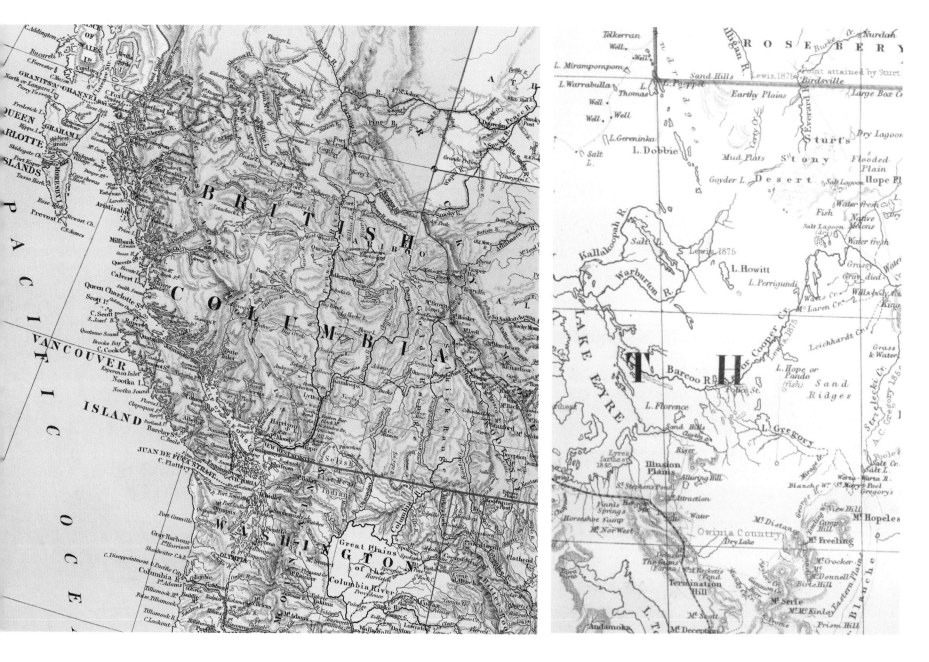

in some of the smaller Caribbean islands, so that in 1912 Stanford was still selling a large-scale topographical map of St. Kitts that had been first published in 1828, and a map of Barbados produced in 1846 by the distinguished South American explorer Sir Robert Schomburgk. These were not Stanford maps, but he had acquired the remaining stock of them. British interest in South America was slight, but from the 1870s onwards there was considerable emigration to, and capital investment in, Argentina, which therefore received its own map in the folio *London Atlas,* while British Guiana was the subject of a large separate map of 1875 at a scale of 1:586,080, again from earlier surveys by Schomburgk, who had explored much of the Orinoco region and the Roraima plateau. This map is annotated with detailed notes on the location of the exotic hardwoods which formed the chief export of Guiana. There was a long-standing dispute between British Guiana and Venezuela about the location of their boundary, and this was the subject of a special Stanford map published in 1898, extensively researched by John Bolton. International arbitration in 1899 handed down a decision broadly favourable to Britain.

Another great South American explorer whose maps were drawn by Stanford was the mountaineer Edward Whymper, who scaled the Andean volcanoes Chimborazo and Cotopaxi in 1880. Whymper's book *Travels Among the Great Andes of the Equator,* 1892, was illustrated with a fine sketch-map of his route, and detailed plans of the summits. One ancient cartographic survival, which Stanford still retained until the second edition of the folio *London Atlas* in 1893, was a map of the Falkland Islands. The islands had been British since 1765, and were inhabited by several hundred sheep farmers, mostly of Scots origin. This map was in fact a copy of a nautical chart drawn from surveys made as long ago as 1832 by Captain Robert Fitzroy of HMS *Beagle,* the ship on which Charles Darwin had made his great scientific voyage to South America and the Pacific.

AUSTRALASIA

In 1840 Charles Sturt, pioneer of Australian exploration, wrote, "Let any man lay the map of Australia before him and regard the blank upon its surface, and then let me ask him if it would not be an honourable achievement to be the first to set foot in its centre." This summed up the geographical challenge which Australia presented to its European settlers: they had occupied perhaps five per cent of its land area in a narrow coastal strip, while the vast continental interior remained as unexplored as that of Africa. Between 1845 and 1875, however, Australian history accelerated dramatically: the population soared from 350,000 to 1.5 million; the penal labour system was abolished; four new embryo states were established; valuable

OPPOSITE FAR LEFT: **Part of the map of British Columbia from the 1887** *London Atlas*; **south-east of the letter A of Columbia, is Mount Stanford, named in Stanford's honour.**

OPPOSITE RIGHT: **Section of the map of south-central Australia from the** *London Atlas* **of 1887. The map is sprinkled with important historical notes on the early explorers, e.g., "Wills's body found here".**

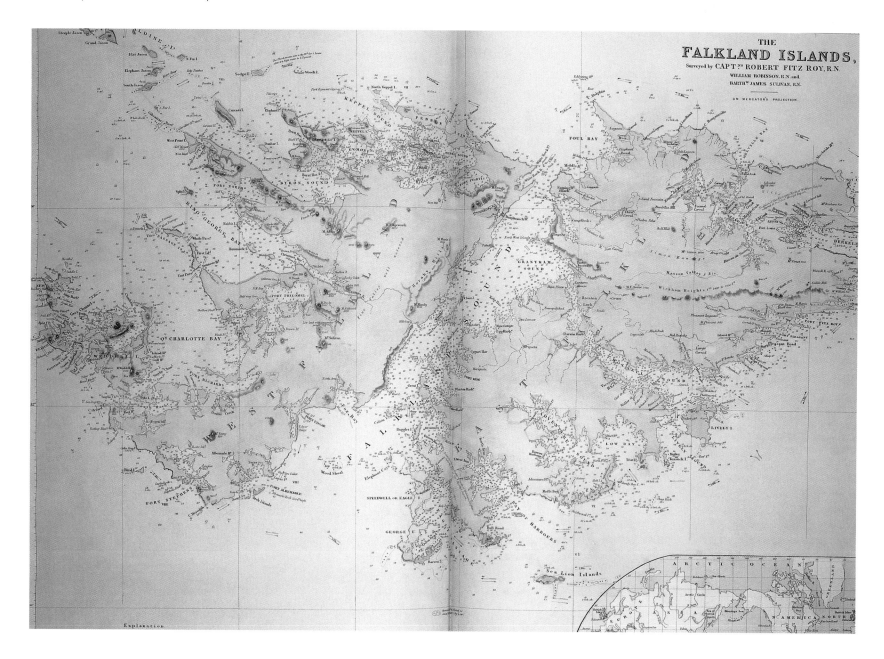

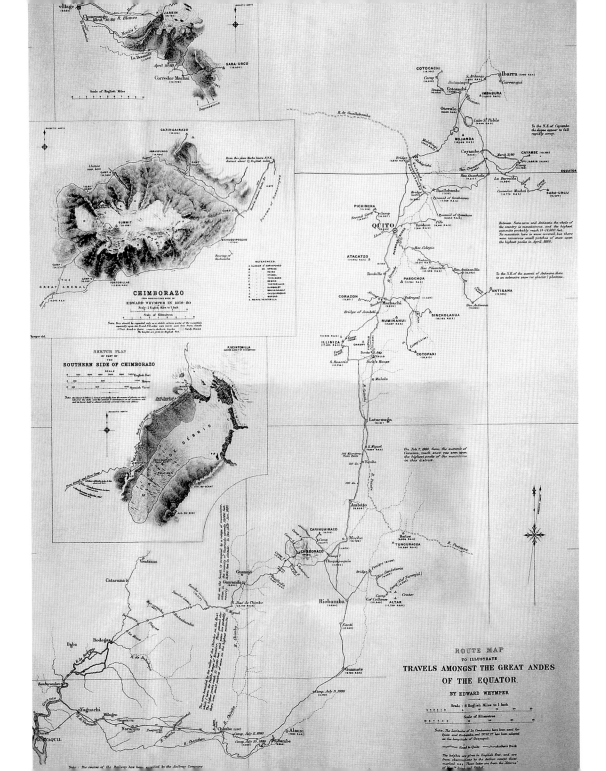

OPPOSITE: **The Falkland Islands, from the 1887** *London Atlas*, **a very old chart, based on the surveys made by Fitzroy of the** *Beagle* **in the 1830s.**

LEFT: **Map of Edward Whymper's travels in the Andes, with sketches of the summit of Chimborazo, included in Whymper's book** *Travels Among the Great Andes*, **1892.**
The Bodleian Library

91

mineral resources were discovered; and the continent was finally crossed and recrossed in search of new pasturage and natural resources. At the price of great personal suffering, the explorers, beginning with Sturt himself, and including Burke and Wills, Stuart, Gregory, Warburton, Eyre, and Forest, dispelled any hopes that the interior held great inland lakes or rich forests, for much of the centre and west of the continent was found to be desert so arid as to be quite uninhabitable; it became clear that settlement would be largely restricted to the south-east quarter.

As early as 1853 Saunders and Stanford had published a map of the Australian goldfields, the first to be discovered in New South Wales and more especially Victoria. Later, Stanford used the topographical data gathered by the Surveyor-General's office to publish maps of each of the colonies, maps which were of widely different characters. Those of Victoria and New South Wales were dense with settlements, administrative divisions, new railways, and the well-mapped topographical features of the Great Dividing Range. Those of South and Western Australia on the other hand displayed little more than the coasts and those strips of territory which marked the passage of the explorers. This contrast was heightened in probably the finest maps of Australia published in the nineteenth century, Stanford's *Library Map of Australia,* at a scale of 1:1.6 million, drawn in nine separate sheets, and measuring when assembled a massive 102 inches x 78 inches, calculated to overawe any visitors to the commercial or government offices where it hung. But in practice much of the continent was still impossible to map: it contained no great rivers or lakes, no alpine ranges, and no chains of new cities. For this reason one of the most interesting features of these maps is their array of notes of the explorers' routes and observations, notes such as "Warburton's furthest, 1874, low stony hills, no water"; "Impenetrable scrub, Eyre compelled to follow the beach"; "Dark and apparently timbered valley, water courses probable"; "Splendid grass, natives numerous"; "Flag planted by Stuart, July 25, 1862"; "Burke's body found"; "Wills' body found". These evocative notes are a direct link with the heroic and arduous years of exploration in the great Australian wildernesses. With the discovery of copper and gold in southern and western Australia, Stanford published in 1895 a map of the western goldfields, and in 1899 a geological map of South Australia.

In the Pacific region, among the detailed island maps which Stanford published were those of the Fiji archipelago, a British colony from 1874 following the success of British missionaries, and of Borneo, part of which was governed by the British North Borneo Company chartered in 1881 to exploit the rich gold and oil reserves. In 1904 Stanford added a map of the Antarctic regions to his folio *London Atlas* series, undoubtedly responding to the public interest in Scott's first *Discovery* expedition of 1901–04. In successive editions of this map the continental topography begins to emerge from the expanse of empty whiteness.

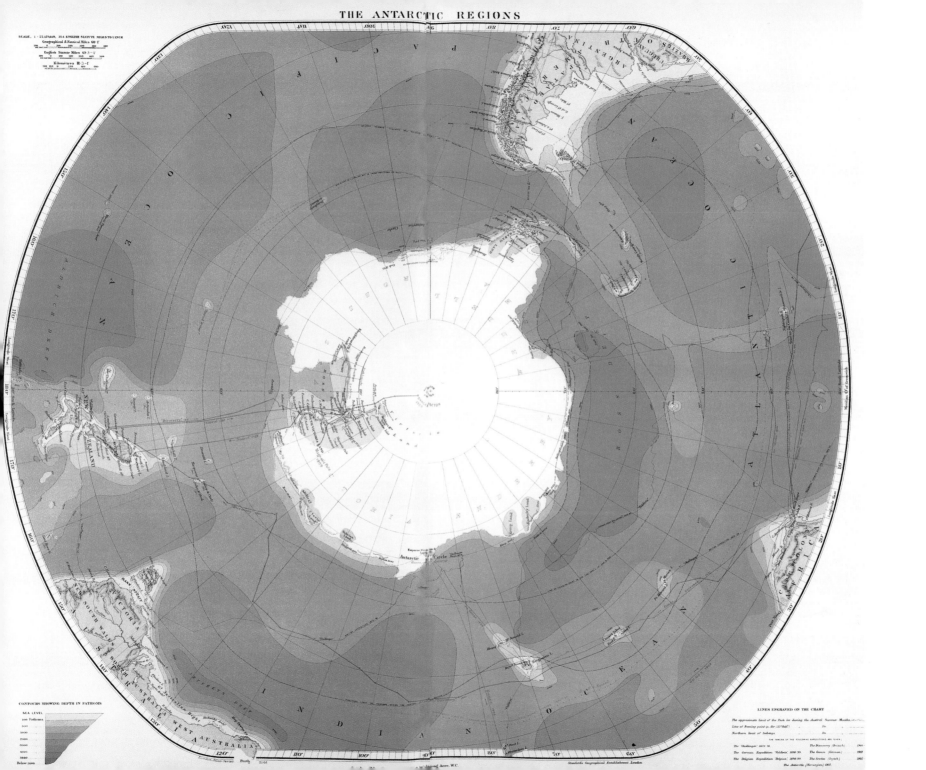

THE ANTARCTIC REGIONS

OPPOSITE: *Map of the Countries Round the North Pole,* **from the** *London Atlas* **of 1887. The notes in red chart the progress of Arctic exploration from Davis and Frobisher in the 1560s to Greely in the 1880s.**

The furthest points south reached by the much earlier expeditions of Bellinghausen, Ross, Wilkes and D'Urville are marked in black, while the tracks of the new generation of Antarctic explorers beginning in the 1890s are shown in red. Like the other maps in this series, this map was sold separately and was therefore kept continually up dated. This is a source of confusion to modern bibliographers, owing to Stanford's practice of leaving the *Atlas* title-page unaltered, while revising the maps. Thus a copy of the *Atlas* bearing the date 1904 on its title-page may well contain an Antarctic map showing Shackleton's furthest south of 1909, or even Amundsen's and Scott's names on the Pole itself, which they did not reach until 1912.

The aim of this survey has been to build up a picture of the impressive range of Stanford's international mapping activities, to show how the firm responded to events throughout the world, especially in regions of direct British involvement. But the maps discussed here were far from exhausting Stanford's map publishing activities. Much of this geographical data was recycled into smaller, scaled-down maps and budget-priced atlases. Outline maps and schoolroom maps of most regions of the world were published, as well as a special series of physical or "orographical" maps of the six continents intended for teaching purposes. This series was edited in the early years of the twentieth century by Sir Halford Mackinder, Britain's leading academic geographer. Of course Stanford mapped the British Isles too, not only geographically, but in numerous thematic maps – geological, hydrographical, parliamentary, ecclesiastical and railway. London was the subject of innumerable maps, the most important being the six-inch map of 1862, universally regarded as the most detailed and practical map of the capital to be published in the nineteenth century. This map was used as the base for a number of specially-coloured editions, showing geology, parish boundaries, or new railways. The edition which has received most attention from historians is probably Charles Booth's social map of 1889, showing by detailed colour coding the levels of wealth and poverty to be found in the streets of London. In addition there were the large numbers of special maps commissioned to illustrate books of geography and history, including of course Stanford's own multi-volume *Compendium of Geography and Travel,* and to accompany articles in *The Geographical Journal* of the R.G.S. In all this work Stanford acted as an intermediary between the official sources of topographical data and the public's insatiable demand for practical maps with which to understand their changing world.

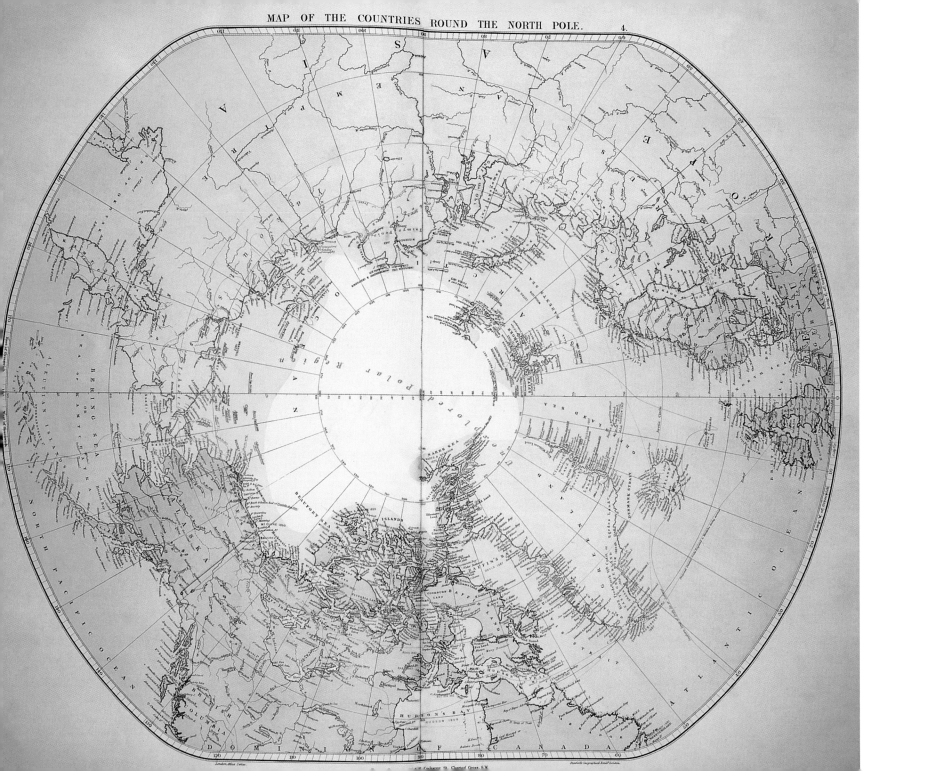

LEFT: **The *Library Map of Europe* 1858, the first of the magnificent continental map-series engraved by A.K.Johnston and coloured by hand after printing.**
The British Library

Part Three **War and Survival**

"The war brings no grist to our mill. We had a very bad year last year, and we are so short-handed that we can hardly keep things going . . . We are doing so little business that we might wish to close down at any time . . . We do not complain; it is the fortune of war; and if we had to close down, it would not be our wish but our necessity."

Edward Stanford wrote these words in the winter of 1915-16, at the mid point of the Great War, the war which was to prove to be a decisive watershed in the firm's history. By the time it ended in 1918 Stanford himself was dead, the business had been decimated by the inevitable restrictions on travel and on the sale of maps, John Bolton had reached the age of 75, and all three of Stanford's sons had commenced military careers and were later to show little enthusiasm for the business. It cannot really be argued that political conditions after the war were fundamentally different from those that existed before it: Britain's international role was still a major one, and the opportunities for mapmaking still existed. But the economic situation had been totally transformed by the war. Military demands and wartime government controls had created an artificial economy, disrupting normal markets and normal methods of working, and this was true not only in Britain, but in all the combatant nations. Once peace came companies large and small struggled to adjust to the free market again, while European governments were crippled with war debts. Stanfords was one of innumerable firms which proved unable to rebuild its operations. Some vital energy had deserted the company. The directors who inherited this immense challenge were either ageing or reluctant businessmen. The publishing programme faltered, while the quality of the maps declined. The firm relied more and more on contract cartographic work, and the splendid Long Acre showroom was emptied and leased to another company. In short, the company lost its way, and many decades would pass before it experienced a renaissance.

Of course this bleak picture conveys only a part of the truth. The firm did survive, and it continued to be identified closely with the sale of Ordnance Survey maps. It carried out a multitude of private mapping activities – for governments, for politicians, for aviators, for historians and for deep-sea fishermen. There were a small number of successful new publications, such as the series of Stanford's *Yachting Charts*, which have flourished now for seventy years. Yet somehow the 1920s and 1930s were for Stanfords what

ABOVE: **A page from Stanford's Catalogue of Maps, Atlases and Books, 1912.**

Diagram 9.—A Set of Ordnance Maps, mounted on linen and folding into leather or morocco boxes.

The Ordnance Survey Maps are now nearly all published, and the public begins to appreciate their excellence and usefulness. Many individuals and institutions find that a set of maps of their own estates, or district, or county, is almost a necessity. A set of cases, as in Diagram 9, forms a most admirable way of keeping a quantity of maps clean, handy, and neat.

DIAGRAM 9.

Libraries, Clubs, Surveyors, and others can have their maps mounted to any size and form desired, and new cases can be made to pattern at any time, if it be found desirable to add to their number. County Councils, Municipal Bodies, Local Boards, and other similar bodies will find a set of maps of their districts mounted in this way invaluable for easy reference.

ABOVE: **Map mounting styles illustrated from Stanford's 1912 catalogue; these maps have been dissected, mounted on cloth and folded into handsome leather cases.**

they were for Britain as a whole – years of uncertainty and bewilderment, years when past glories were clearly felt to be slipping away, and years haunted by the trauma of the Great War.

In July 1912 Edward Stanford had taken the step of converting his business into a Limited Company. Until that date he had been the sole proprietor, taking personally all of the financial risks and gathering all of the rewards. But he was now 56 years old, and his eldest son, Edward Fraser Stanford, had entered the business in 1908. Stanford must have realised that the moment had come when he must separate his own personal finances from those of the firm, and give his son his own stake in it. Stanford awarded himself 20,000 preference shares and 10,000 ordinary shares, and his son 5,000 ordinary shares. There were only two other shareholders: John Bolton with 200, while 100 went to Conrad Wild Hanson. This romantically-named individual was in fact a timid little man, who was Stanford's brother-in-law, and who now became the company secretary, and remained so for 25 years. The change in the firm's status meant that minuted board meetings were now held, and an annual statement of the company's profits becomes available for the first time, although no detailed accounts have survived. In the first year, 1912, profits were £1,904 – in modern values something approaching £100,000. In the following year this had dropped to £1,086, and then in 1914 picked up to £1,322. This would be after Stanford's own remuneration, so the situation was still quite comfortable. But by 1915 came the ravages of the war with a loss of £2,276. The sale of large-scale Ordnance maps had been restricted immediately on the outbreak of the war, while private travel in Europe was virtually halted overnight. Many of Stanford's staff enlisted in the armed forces, and when conscription was introduced in 1916, Stanford's claim that his staff should be treated as engaged in government service was rejected, so that still more were lost.

The army's own mapmaking facility, the Geographical Section of the General Staff, had been developing for thirty years before the outbreak of the war, and was now put seriously to work using the Ordnance Survey's production facilities, so the opportunities for the private map publisher were limited. Stanford moved quickly to produce a number of theatre-of-war maps, covering not only the Western Front but the North Sea, the Baltic, Russia, the Italian Front and Turkey. He also went to great lengths to import official French topographic mapping of the Western Front for resale in England. Stanford also published some strident propaganda maps, including *What Germany Wants*, 1916, which took the form of a world map whose regions were keyed to quotations from Germany's political and military leaders, demanding German occupation of, or access to, about one third of the earth. But the profits from these various war maps went only a small way to replacing the massive loss of other sales. The widespread and naïve optimism that the war would be over in a few months was amply demonstrated when a would-be author wrote to Stanford in October 1914 proposing to write a guidebook to the battlefields of France. Stanford replied grimly that no one could yet foretell when it would be possible to visit those sites, and the whole idea was totally premature.

Stanford's personal fondness for all things German had led him twenty years earlier to choose the word *Zeitgeist* as his telegraphic address, which appeared on all his business stationery; this was now hastily changed to the more neutral *Estanfomaps*. The war also gave him another idea, and he told anyone who would listen that the moment was ripe to shut out the German Baedeker guidebooks and prepare a new English guidebook series, to be launched when the war was over. Stanford had realised long ago that he was not the man to develop the Murray *Handbooks*, and he told the publishers' agent Curtis Brown that he would part with the series for £2,500 if a buyer could be found. This was finally achieved in September 1915 after months of negotiations, but Stanford had in the meantime been intensely irritated because John Murray himself had let it be known that £2,000 had been the price paid for the series in 1901, and, in the difficult climate of 1915 this inevitably became the maximum price which Stanford could now hope for. The buyers were two brothers, Findlay and James Muirhead, who had been the English editors of the Baedeker books, and who now found themselves out of a job. In the hands of the Muirheads, the famous red-covered Murray guides were never relaunched in Britain, but they would eventually be metamorphosed into the *Guides Bleus*, which in turn became the Blue Guides published by Ernest Benn. Stanford received back the £2,000 he had given in 1901, a welcome cash boost to relieve briefly the financial gloom of 1915.

At the outbreak of the war Stanford's three sons enlisted at once. Fraser was already a part-time soldier in the Honourable Artillery Company, and he joined the HAC Battery which served in the Middle East throughout the conflict, while the younger sons, John Keith and Henry Morrant, both went to the Western Front, John in the Suffolk regiment, Morrant in the Royal Horse Artillery. In September 1915 Edward Stanford wrote to a friend, "My second son is home suffering from shell-shock, but going on satisfactorily I think. The youngest is at the front in the west, and my eldest boy is near Aden, a nice handy place for a director of this company." A year earlier Stanford had hoped soon to retire to his home on the Suffolk coast, to hand over the business to Fraser, and to enjoy his weekend shooting. Now he was forced to shoulder the burdens of responsibility again, while his sons stood in daily danger of their lives, and to watch the enterprise which he had built up so successfully slide towards ruin. The strain was too much: he became seriously ill in the winter of 1916–17, and he died on 6 June of that year, aged 61. He was buried at Aldringham in Suffolk. His death had been expected, and Fraser was summoned back to England to be present, and to assume the post of governing director. He knew that he must soon return to the fighting,

ABOVE: **A screen for a gentleman's study, adorned with maps, from Stanford's 1912 catalogue.**

so John Bolton and Stanford's widow Caroline were now appointed directors. In the last full year of the war losses totalled £1,555. It had been discovered that the account with the Ordnance Survey had run into confusion, that sales had considerably exceeded the commission actually paid to the Survey, and that a large deficit would have to be made up, even though the firm was already in debt to its bankers. Moreover, Fraser and the new directors had realised that many of the engraved printing plates, which were theoretically a valuable asset, were old and out of date and must be written off. The future looked bleak, but there was nothing to be done but struggle on, until either the war ended, or closure was forced on them by their bank. Stanford's plight was typical of the map trade as a whole, for we know that the London chart makers Imray were in an even more critical situation, the war having destroyed three-quarters of their business.

Edward Fraser Stanford (1885-1944) had two passions in life, soldiering and horses: running a map-selling business was only his accidental fate. He was sent to Uppingham School, where he joined the cadet corps, and then, while at Lincoln College Oxford, he was a member of the university's mounted infantry from 1904-1907. After Oxford he spent a year at Heidelberg University, continuing his family's German connection, before entering the business in 1908. He joined the Honourable Artillery Company, the elite militia of the City of London, whose Captain-General is always the reigning monarch, and where he gained a reputation as a superb horseman. In World War One he served in Egypt and Mesopotamia, latterly under General Allenby, and was present at all three battles of Gaza. After the war he remained deeply committed to the HAC, and was appointed Master Gunner within the Tower in 1935, and Brevet Lieutenant-Colonel in 1936. It is beyond question that Fraser's heart was in the army, in riding and shooting near his home at Westerham in Kent, and that, by temperament or training, this was not the man to rebuild a struggling business.

But his period of control started well, for in the event the company did survive the war, as did all the three brothers. Stanfords then shared in that extraordinary burst of business prosperity which followed the war, when the pent up demand for consumer goods of all kinds fuelled a boom in Britain's economy through 1919 and 1920. In the eighteen months following the war Stanfords recorded a staggering profit of £6,663, after years of crippling losses. It must have seemed briefly that the great days had returned. The directors received dividends, the staff were awarded war bonuses, debts were paid off, a new electrical generator and printing-press were bought, and a new edition of the folio *London Atlas* was contemplated. This boom was short-lived, however, and by 1921 the British economy had entered a long period of stagnation and rising unemployment. In fact, throughout the 1920s Stanfords continued to achieve quite healthy profits, only once falling below £2,000 in a year. Yet something had changed profoundly in the business atmosphere since the war: some loss of confidence and loss of vision seemed to paralyse the company,

OPPOSITE: **Edward Fraser Stanford with his first love – the army; he is leading members of the Honourable Artillery Company as they parade before the new king, George VI, in 1936.**

EDWARD STANFORD, LTD.

12, 13, & 14, LONG ACRE, W.C.

(FORMERLY AT 6, 7, & 8, AND 55, CHARING CROSS, AND 26 AND 27, COCKSPUR STREET, S.W.)

DEPARTMENTS

Publishing. Maps and books arranged for and published. Estimates and terms on application.

Map Selling. This department includes the productions of every map publisher of repute both at home and abroad, as well as the publications of the various foreign and colonial Governments, and the Ordnance and Geological Survey Maps.

Map Mounting. This is done on the premises by skilled workmen. See pages 88 to 105 of this Catalogue.

Map Engraving. This department includes drawing, lithography, and engraving of all kinds. Edward Stanford's large collection of copyright maps is available for transfers for book illustration, etc. Estimates given.

Books. The best Guide-books, Books of Travel, Memoirs of the Geological Survey, and all Standard Geographical and Geological Works are kept in stock. Any book can be obtained.

Passport Agency.

EDWARD STANFORD, LTD.

LONDON AGENTS FOR THE SALE OF THE ORDNANCE AND GEOLOGICAL SURVEY MAPS, AND THE MAPS PUBLISHED BY THE GEOGRAPHICAL SECTION, GENERAL STAFF, WAR OFFICE.

AGENTS FOR THE INDIAN TRIGONOMETRICAL SURVEY MAPS, THE ADMIRALTY CHARTS, THE PUBLICATIONS OF THE ROYAL GEOGRAPHICAL SOCIETY, THE ROYAL METEOROLOGICAL SOCIETY, THE ROYAL SANITARY INSTITUTE, THE GEOLOGISTS' ASSOCIATION, ETC.

ABOVE: **Stanford's prospectus, describing the departments of the business, and the official agencies held, 1916.**

for these profits were not reinvested in new publications. The publishing programme contracted to a fraction of what it had been in the year 1900. The great folio atlas in its promised new edition never appeared; the Library series of reference maps were not updated and reissued; the many large-scale regional maps of parts of Africa, Australia, Asia and Canada were replaced by small-scale atlas maps, indeed in the 1930s Stanfords was still selling sheets from the *London Atlas* series which had been first published in the 1880s. Stanford's role as an intermediary between worldwide survey authorities and the map-buying public seems to have largely withered away. In 1920 John Bolton went into semi-retirement, to be succeeded as chief cartographer and then as director by Ernest Thomas, who had himself joined Stanfords in 1884. Bolton was still working part-time when he died in 1925 at the age of 81.

In 1926 the company determined to buy the freehold of the Long Acre premises from the Stanford family for the sum of £28,000, made possible through a massive bank loan. This event represented a splendid windfall for the family, but there must have been many occasions in the following decade when the company bitterly regretted taking on the burden of this loan. This transaction came about in a curious way. By March 1926 Fraser had come to the conclusion that the retail showroom was not operating as profitably as it might, largely because Long Acre was not then seen as a fashionable shopping area, littered as it often was with fruit and vegetables and rubbish from the nearby Covent Garden Market. Fraser proposed instead that they should lease a separate showroom back in the Stanford heartland of Charing Cross, and that the ground floor of Long Acre could in turn be sublet. Under the terms of Edward Stanford's will trustees had been appointed to administer his estate in the family's interest, and they, as controllers of the Long Acre premises, objected to this plan. The solution in Fraser's eyes was to buy the Long Acre site outright, so that the company would be free to do with it as it wished. This was agreed, but it proved to be a serious mistake. Stanfords took a 25-year lease on a former Lyons coffee-house at 29-30 Charing Cross (later renumbered as 43 Whitehall) at £1,500 per year, and leased the ground floor of Long Acre as a car showroom at £1,000 per year. But their tenant soon went into liquidation, and over the following fifteen years, time and energy which should have been devoted to mapmaking, were spent in looking for new tenants, who all proved unsatisfactory, while the retail sales from the new showroom never achieved the hoped-for levels.

Then in 1929-30 came the economic depression following the world-wide stock-market crashes. No sector of the economy was immune, and after fourteen years of profits, Stanfords recorded a loss of almost £2,000 in 1932, and over £3,000 in 1933. The property loan was converted to a slightly less burdensome mortgage (advanced by Christ's Hospital). In January 1933 Caroline, the widow of Edward

Stanford, died, and her shares passed to her three sons. For two years, 1934 and 1935, modest profits were achieved, but then from 1936 onwards some kind of financial crisis seems to have engulfed the company. Profit and loss figures were not recorded "pending further investigation". There were large discrepancies in the Ordnance Survey account, and inter-departmental charging became thoroughly confused. There was an awareness that the board needed to be strengthened in order to get to grips with the firm's problems, but the chosen appointees were solicitors and accountants, never publishers, or mapmakers or retailers. Several times in the late 1930s, the Ordnance Survey account could only be paid with the help of an overdraft from an understanding bank. Fraser's son later recalled the gloom at the family breakfast table during these years, as his father prepared for the daily struggle with a floundering business. It is hard to resist drawing an image of Stanfords at this time as resembling the nation in miniature: struggling with a hostile environment, menaced by forces it could not understand, and looking into a bleak and wholly unknown future.

What of the publishing programme during these years? Strikingly absent were the large reference maps of the continents, and the detailed survey maps of the regions of British interest which had both characterised Stanford's pre-war map publishing. The peace settlement following the war offered an obvious challenge to the mapmaker, and Stanford responded with the *Peace Conference Atlas* of 1919, which displayed the changed boundaries in Europe, and the new nations which had emerged from the ruins of the Austro-Hungarian and Turkish Empires; the League of Nations mandated territories were also shown, as were Germany's lost colonies in Africa and the Pacific. A new edition of the folio *London Atlas* never appeared, but instead a quarto world atlas was published in 1926 entitled *The Whitehall Atlas*, a reference to the new showroom at Charing Cross-Whitehall. The maps in this atlas were naturally on a smaller scale, and were noticeably inferior to the earlier series. Demand for maps of individual countries – Scandinavia, Greece, South Africa, India or Ceylon – was fulfilled by the sale of single sheets of the *London Atlas* series, which were kept up to date and reprinted in small quantities. There seems to have been a general decline in standards in map production in the 1920s and 1930s among all publishers, perhaps due to a desire to print more cheaply and more quickly. In Stanford's case the long-postponed transition from hand colouring to printed colour now resulted in the loss of the clear, luminous colours which had distinguished their pre-war maps.

Patterns of travel in this period are difficult to assess. There was evidently a huge pent up urge to escape from the post-war wasteland of 1920s Britain. These were the years when it was almost obligatory for writers to free their imagination by travelling in the Mediterranean, Iceland, Africa, Arabia or Central Asia – anywhere out of a grey, exhausted Europe, out of the shadow of the war. There was a flowering of

RIGHT: **A remarkably detailed map of the rivers of the British Isles, included in the 1887 *London Atlas*.**

English travel writing in scores of books with titles beginning *Into the Heart of . . . , Into Unknown . . . , Journey Beyond . . . , Into Lost . . . , South of . . . , North of . . .* and so on. There was a definite sense that travel was liberating because it was an encounter with the unknown, the exotic or the threatening. Mountaineering and seafaring literature offered an escape from the humdrum safety of England into a world of loneliness and danger in the Himalayas or the Arctic. But this was a literary movement, an intellectual fashion, with no great commercial impact, for the era of mass foreign travel had not yet arrived in which a map publisher would thrive.

The book publishing programme had been allowed to wither, and Stanfords made no contribution to this literary movement, so that travel narratives of this kind were published by John Murray, Macmillan, Longman and the other mainstream publishers. Stanford's geographical publications at this time were of a drier and more factual kind, such as the publications of the Royal Meteorological Society, or indices to the war cemeteries in Belgium.

Stanfords continued to publish a wide range of maps of London and of the British Isles, but what they signally failed to do was to develop a series of regional maps for tourists, motorists and cyclists under the Stanford name. The Ordnance Survey, John Bartholomew and George Philip all did precisely that in the 1920s, and Stanfords lost its chance to establish its name in a fast-growing market. Instead Stanfords secured a commission to produce a series of small-scale motoring maps for the *Daily Mail.* Although this commission involved large print-runs, the price was very low and profits were small. The rival publishers, John Bartholomew and still more George Philip, came to dominate the atlas market, with a range of publications at prices from 6d upwards, with which Stanford could not compete. It seems clear that, rather than producing risk publications for the open market, it was contract cartography which sustained Stanfords between the wars. An outstanding example was the atlas which Stanford compiled in 1926 to accompany the arbitration which ended the Labrador boundary question. The province of Quebec and the self-governing colony of Newfoundland had long disputed possession of a large tract of the Labrador coast, and Stanford was commissioned by the British and Canadian governments to assemble a collection of historical maps of eastern Canada from 1656 to 1912, in order to build up a body of evidence concerning the boundary. Almost fifty maps were reproduced from originals in the British Museum, with notes by James de Villiers, the Museum's map curator. The overall conclusion, upheld by the official arbitration, was that the boundary should be placed near the headwaters of those rivers which flowed into the Atlantic, and a huge swathe of land to the east of that watershed was consequently awarded to Newfoundland. Commission map publishing for individual customers on a shared profit basis became less common than it

RIGHT: **A graphic map of the physical geography of the British Isles, from the 1887** *London Atlas.*

had been before the war, and only a few examples are to be found, such as a map of railways and minerals resources of Siberia of 1922, edited by Colonel de Metz, a French officer and scientist.

A completely new field of mapping was opened up by the growth of aviation after the war. Early fliers had to use whatever maps they could find, navigating entirely by landmarks, but by the late 1920s many countries had begun to publish purpose-drawn aeronautical charts. These marked airfields, and gave details of their radio beacons, emphasised water features to aid night flying, included compass roses and magnetic variations, and they highlighted hazards such as power lines. Stanfords quickly developed a specialist business in preparing such maps by editing them into strip form to show any specific route, sometimes adding distances or other information by hand. These strip maps could be concertina folded for easy handling in an aircraft, and were exactly the kind of maps which Stanfords supplied to Amy Johnson for her famous solo flight to Australia in 1930. Another speciality of a more traditional kind was the hunt map – a composite made by cutting and joining one-inch Ordnance Survey maps and hand colouring the boundaries of a hunt. These maps would be dissected, mounted on linen and folded into a small leather case; this was skilled work which gave high added value to the cheap paper maps. Of course Stanfords could also draw special maps to order; an example that was long remembered in the firm was a huge sketch-map of the western world commissioned by Lloyd George in 1939 demonstrating the growing power of Germany. It was to be displayed at a public meeting, and was reportedly thirty feet across. By contrast in 1922 Stanford drew what were perhaps the smallest maps ever published – a series for a tiny atlas to be placed in Queen Mary's famous doll's house in Windsor Castle. There were a dozen maps, each just two inches square, of the world's main regions, although Europe at that size evidently defeated the mapmaker's skill. These maps were later reprinted in Stanford's *British Empire Diary* as a tiny book designed to slip into the waistcoat pocket.

Surely the most original and idiosyncratic of these commission maps were those produced for Albert Close, a Canadian engineer who settled in England and whose career was connected with Stanfords for forty years. Close was a seafarer who first dedicated himself to producing reliable, inexpensive charts for Britain's sea-fishing industry, and *Close's Fisherman's Charts* were published from around 1910 to the 1950s. They were based on Admiralty charts, supplemented by Close's own data which he collected over years of active research around Britain's coastline. He was a highly combative character who came into frequent conflict with the Admiralty over the question of copyright. He strongly defended the view that the Admiralty surveys had been carried out at public expense, and that the public, and in particular the maritime community, had therefore a right to make use of them. Close's *Handy Wheel-House Chart-Book*,

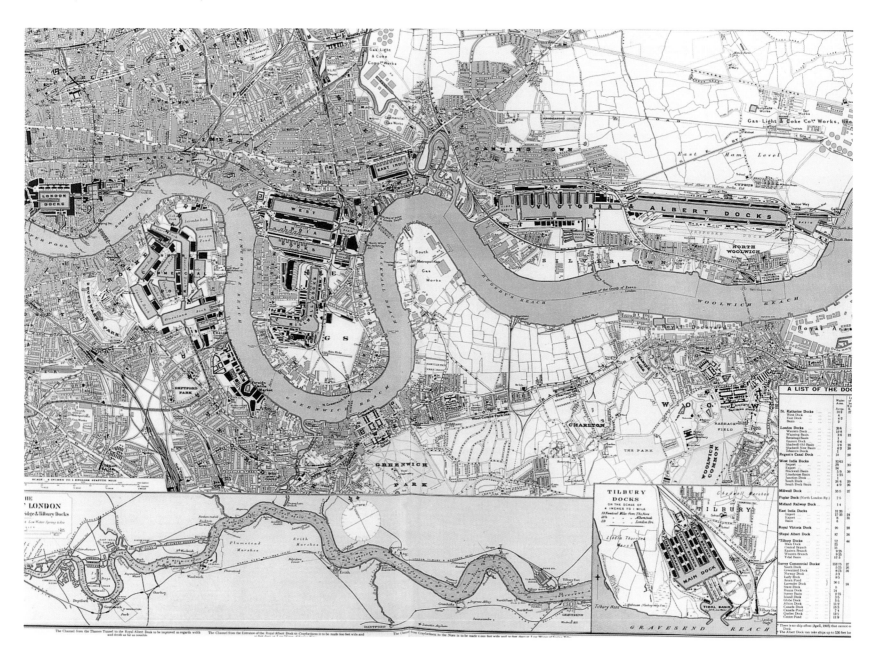

1920, was an atlas containing more than fifty coastal and harbour charts, printed and sold by Stanfords. Close's aim of selling his charts cheaply meant that he never became rich, indeed he was often in financial difficulty, and more than once offered to sell the series to Stanford, who declined. The fishing charts were only one aspect of Close's activities. He was intensely patriotic, and after the war he devoted many years to the production of a series of extraordinary historical maps including *The Naval War in the North Sea*, 1921, and *The British Empire at Bay on the Western Front*, 1922. These large maps were densely packed with text, images, biographies, quotations and statistics, and they formed virtually a visual encyclopedia of the history of the war, emphasising in particular the suffering and heroism of the ordinary seaman, merchant as well as Royal Naval, and the callous brutality of the German forces, especially the U-Boat commanders. The third string to Close's bow was his religion: he was a passionate anti-Catholic, a leading member of the Protestant Truth Society, and author of many polemical works with titles like *The Hand of God and Satan in Modern History, or Antichrist and his Ten Kingdoms*. Many of these books were illustrated with highly graphic maps showing the historical threat posed by Catholicism to Protestant Europe. Close was surely one of the oddest and most colourful minor characters in the history of twentieth-century mapmaking.

The Stanford family had become, partly by historical accident, an intensely military family, and neither they nor any of their senior staff had any connection with seafaring. This makes it all the more surprising that one of the best known of all the Stanford publications should be the series of yachting charts, launched in the gloom of the 1930s, and still flourishing today, although now independently owned. They were the brainchild of Captain Oswald Watts, a retired merchant navy officer, who had worked as an editor for Imray, the commercial chart publishers, and for Thomas Reed, publishers of the nautical almanac. Captain Watts later opened a well-known yacht chandlers in London's Albemarle Street. Watts approached Stanford with the idea of a new series of charts of British coastal waters, covering limited areas, and tailored very much for the weekend yachtsman. Watts himself edited the charts, and they were sold folded into attractive covers, beginning with *The Solent* in 1932 and *The Thames Estuary* in 1933. They were an immediate success and a further half-dozen titles appeared before the war halted their progress. Captain Watts also inaugurated Stanford maps of England's inland waterways, and of the River Thames "for oarsmen and yachtsmen", maps which were frequently revised and reprinted.

These charts were perhaps the most valuable permanent legacy of the otherwise grim years of the 1930s. By early 1939 it seemed certain that history was about to repeat itself, and that Britain was once again to be plunged into war with Germany. As the decade crumbled to its inglorious end, Stanfords were busy converting their basement into an air raid shelter, trying to terminate the lease on the unsuccessful Whitehall

OPPOSITE: **Map of the Port of London, from the third edition of the *London Atlas*, 1904.**

OVER PAGE: ***The Naval War in the North Sea.* One of Albert Close's huge, historical charts on which he laboured for years, and which Stanfords printed and sold for him. Close issued a companion piece, *The British Empire at Bay on the Western Front.***

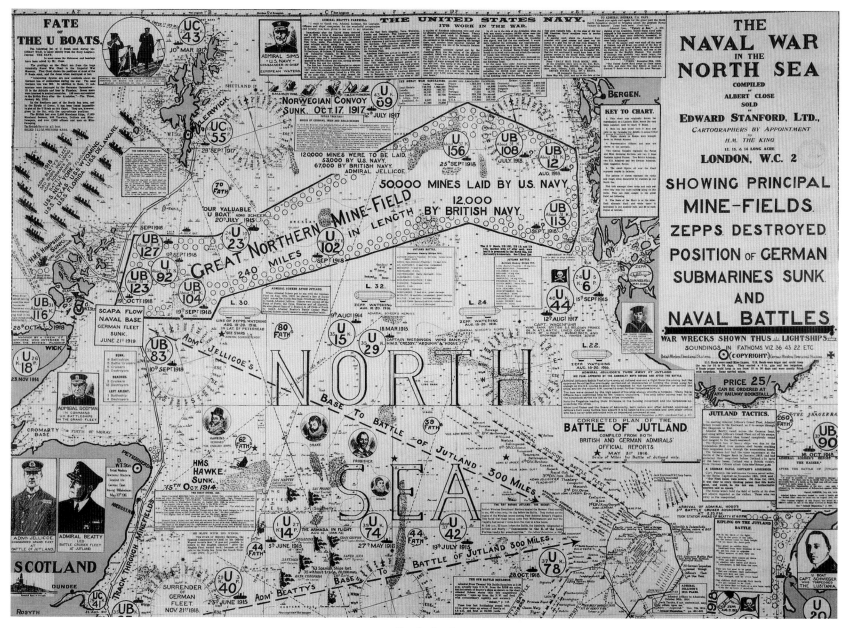

North sheet

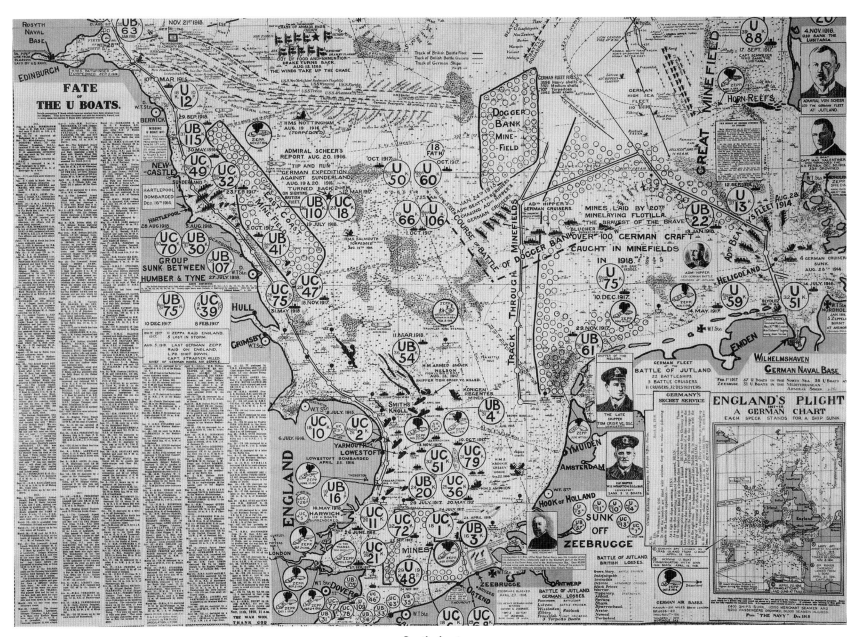

South sheet

shop, borrowing money to pay the Ordnance Survey commission-stock account, and wondering how the firm could possibly survive once more the disruption of trade and the loss of staff that war would bring.

Once again Stanford's battles were emblematic of the nation's as a whole. On the night of 16-17 April 1941, the Long Acre premises took a direct hit from an incendiary bomb, and the top two floors of the building were virtually destroyed by fire. At first it was feared that thousands of sheets of Ordnance Survey maps had been lost, but stacked paper does not burn easily, and most of the stock was found to be safe, although for years afterwards Ordnance maps were being sold with charred edges. Stanfords issued far fewer war maps between 1939 and 1945 than they had during World War One. The battle zones of western Russia were the subject of a 1941 map, while a map of the Pacific war zone appeared in 1942. General small-scale maps of Italy, 1943, and France and Germany, 1944, were aimed at those wishing to follow the war news from those theatres. Once again though from 1941 to 1944 the company's losses mounted inexorably, and then in March 1944, Fraser Stanford died suddenly aged 59. It was an uncanny rerun of history, for he died, just as his father had done, in the midst of a disastrous war, at a relatively early age, and leaving the firm without proper leadership. Fraser had been engaged during 1943 to 1944 on secret war work involving map planning for Operation 'Overlord' – the D-Day landing – work that he carried out in a cell in Wormwood Scrubs Prison, which had been partly converted for the use of military intelligence staff.

Fraser was succeeded as governing director by his younger brother, John Keith Stanford (1892-1971), the last member of the family to run the business. J.K. – as he was familiarly known, but always Colonel Stanford to his colleagues and employees – was a complex character: private, restless, unconventional and scholarly, he became a writer of considerable skill. He was deeply a countryman, passionate about birds, both as subjects of study and as objects to be shot at, and was totally out of place in the business world in which he now found himself. Those who knew him best thought of him as a kind of aristocratic gypsy. He had gained a scholarship to Rugby, and went on as a scholar to St.John's College Oxford, where, owing to illness during his finals he took a rather poor degree in classics in 1913. One year after leaving Oxford he joined the Suffolk Regiment and was sent to the Western Front, where he was twice wounded and was awarded the Military Cross. When the war was over he joined the Indian Civil Service and from 1919-38 he was an administrator in Burma. He was awarded the OBE for his part in quelling the Burma rebellion of 1930-31, and became District Commissioner for Myitkyina. He later referred briefly to the soul-destroying grimness and tedium of this life, but certain aspects of the country fascinated him: he gazed longingly towards the northern mountains which fringed his district, and he studied the bird and animal species brought to him by travellers. One wonders if J.K. ever met the young George Orwell, who was a very out-of-place officer in the Burma police from 1922-27.

In 1938 J.K. returned to England and took up the burden of helping his brother to run Stanfords. But almost at once his chance came to explore the mountains of Burma: he was invited to join an expedition organised by the American Museum of Natural History, whose brief was to collect as many specimens of animals and plant life as they could from this virtually unexplored region. He was packed and ready to go in September 1938 when the Munich crisis erupted, and he waited, believing war to be imminent, finally sailing a couple of weeks later when the crisis eased. The Burmese expedition lasted six months, but again within months of his return to England business had to take second place, for war was declared, and he immediately rejoined the army at the age of forty-seven. He was in France in 1940, in the Middle East in 1941-43, and in Europe in 1944-45, rising to the rank of Lieutenant-Colonel. He was periodically in London during these years, but the attention he was able to give to Stanfords was absolutely minimal. When the war was over he longed to settle in the country and live by his pen. He had already published *The Birds of Northern Burma*, 1939, *Far Ridges*, 1944, his account of the Burmese expedition, and *The Twelfth*, 1944, the first of his comic novels about the country sports circles in which he moved. After Fraser's death, and in the particularly bleak conditions of post-war London, the prospect of trying to rebuild a crippled business for which he had little feeling utterly appalled him, and J.K. decided to get out.

By the summer of 1946 he was negotiating with George Philip with a view to selling the business. Philips was a solid, long-established map publisher, even older than Stanfords, who had wisely chosen to invest in atlases and tourist maps for mass-market and educational sale, and they had come through the difficult years since 1914 much better than Stanfords. Although still a family firm, Philips had a larger and more broadly-based management team, and they understood the need for innovation. Like Stanfords they had a London showroom – in Fleet Street, in the same building that John Murray had once occupied. They also possessed a large cartographic print and production facility at Willesden in west London. They had an extensive publishing programme and a strong presence in the book trade. They were a national and indeed an international company, where Stanfords was small, parochial and Victorian by comparison. What did Philips gain in Stanfords? They gained a famous name, a specialist map retailing business which included the valuable Ordnance Survey agency, and a large freehold property. What they did not gain, for they had created it already, was a modern world-wide map base which could be endlessly spun out into atlases large and small, together with a trade presence to sell their publications. They eliminated a

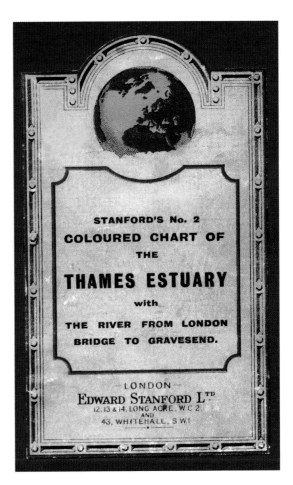

ABOVE: **The cover of the 1938 edition of Stanford's yachtsman's** *Coloured Chart of the Thames Estuary*; **this was the most successful new map series published in the inter-war years.**

RIGHT: **A section of the 1938 Thames Estuary chart.**

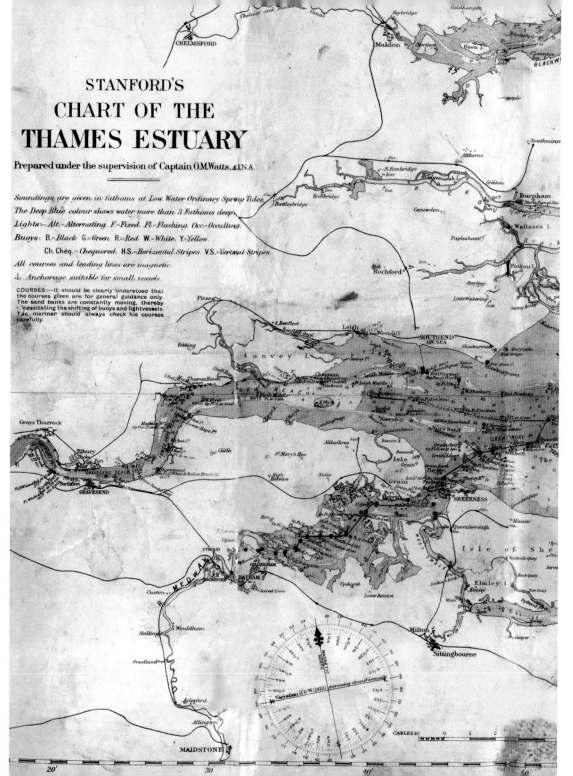

rival, and perhaps they foresaw that Stanford's shop, if properly managed, could provide a steady cash flow which might even out the notorious troughs in any publisher's finances. In November 1946 the deal was complete, and all Stanfords' shares and assets were transferred to Philips, for a reputed (though unconfirmed) £60,000. J.K. was a very relieved man. His younger brother Morrant was now a Brigadier, and had always refused to involve himself in the business. Fraser and J.K. both had sons who were in their twenties, who had now opted for military or farming careers, seeing no future for themselves in what they regarded as the tedious and near-Dickensian world of Long Acre.

Thus the Stanford family relinquished the enterprise which had been launched 93 years earlier by their grandfather. They were driven to this course of action by two quite distinct forces. First the Great War, and the economic conditions which followed it, had disrupted the niche market in which Stanford had flourished, and had fatally weakened the business, so that it now loomed in their minds as a problem and a burden, and not as a source of wealth or professional satisfaction. But secondly, all three sons had found their lives turned by their education and by the war into new channels, and they themselves had lost the desire and the skill to rebuild or even to continue it. Personally and socially they had outgrown the business, outgrown any desire to earn their living "in trade". It was a historical and personal break with the past, and one which had been typical of so many British businesses.

At Christmastime in 1946, Philips hosted a dinner-dance to which the Stanford staff were also invited. The Philips men gazed curiously at their new colleagues, while the Stanford personnel wondered nervously what their future would be. J.K. continued as a kind of honorary chairman for a few years, while the executive director of Stanfords was now R. Lassel Philip, soon to become chairman of the parent company too. As soon as he decently could, J.K. forsook the grind of office life, and fulfilled his ambition of becoming a professional writer, living mainly on the Hampshire downs near Kingsclere. A stream of novels and non-fiction works followed throughout the 1950s and 1960s; he contributed many articles to *Blackwood's Magazine*; and he wrote a column called "The Changing Year" for *The Field* from 1952 to 1961. His books are idiosyncratic, humorous and stylish, but limited in their range of subjects. Many passages in his writings suggest that his was really a poetic spirit, imprisoned in the social world of the country gentleman, the officer, the retired sahib. His greatest praise was to say of someone, "He knew how things should be done properly." He was happy to be free, to be in control of his own life and future, and no one can blame him for that; but was there now a future for Stanfords? This question had to be faced not because the company was no longer in the family's hands – but because it had been taken over by a trade rival.

ABOVE: **John Keith Stanford, the last family owner of the business; "J.K." to his family, but always "Colonel Stanford" within the firm.**

ABOVE: **Conduit Court, Long Acre around 1920; Stanford's wall is on the left. "The Bird in Hand" was the local for generations of Stanfordians; after its closure the trendier "Lamb and Flag" in Rose Street took its place.**

Part Four **Renaissance**

To summarise the years from 1950 to 1980 as a period of drift in Stanfords' history would be unfair to the many able people who worked for the company and who could point to some real achievements. But it was probably inevitable that Stanfords would lose much of its identity, for it existed now in name only. Stanfords' cartographic activity was gradually absorbed into Philips' larger one. The printing presses were removed from Long Acre, draftsmen were transferred to Willesden, and cartographic work produced in the Stanford name was carried out by Philips facilities. All this was sound commercial sense, and moreover the parent company itself was not static, but was expanding its activities. It acquired other map and book publishers; it acquired a globe-making business; it undertook joint publications with overseas partners in Europe, America and Australia; it created a large book distribution service for other publishers; it separated its property holdings into a separate company. All this was natural dynamic growth, but it meant that little time or energy was devoted to developing a special strategy for Stanfords, which accounted for less than 10 per cent of Philip's total business, and was left to mark time. Philips had been correct in their belief that Stanfords could contribute immensely to their cash flow: general sales in these years were good, and the new owners had realised that the Long Acre premises were significantly undervalued, so that a new mortgage arranged in 1950 provided a rich injection of cash for the parent company.

Philips did indeed make some initial efforts to rebuild Stanfords. The war-damaged building was repaired, and some old publications were revived. At the end of the war Stanfords had optimistically decided to revise and reprint some of the great *Library* maps: *Europe* and *North America* had appeared in 1945, and Philips agreed to reissue *Africa* in 1949. But the costs of revision and reprinting were too high, the sales were disappointing, and the experiment was stopped. They were replaced by a smaller Stanford series of "General Maps" of Europe, Asia, North America, Malaya, the Middle East and so on. These were smaller, cheaper, serviceable maps, but undistinguished compared with their monumental Victorian predecessors. A number of miscellaneous Stanford travel books were published in the late 1940s, on Portugal, Persia, Mexico and East Africa, but these books had an uncertain identity: they were not practical guidebooks, nor were they imaginative evocations of their subjects. Sales were meagre, and the series was allowed to die quietly. The one area in which the Stanford name was felt to be really strong enough to exploit was in nautical publishing. The range of yachting charts was steadily extended, and new titles relating to inland waterways and canoeing were added. Later, in the early 1970s, Philips would create a new publishing imprint – "Stanford Maritime" – for a range of books on leisure yachting, boat building and navigation. Only in the maritime field was there a distinct plan and a determination to build a publishing identity.

In a sense, the sale to Philips, and the consequent absorption of Stanford's mapmaking activity into that of Philips, finally resolved Stanford's long-standing uncertainty about its role as map publisher. Throughout the 1920s and 1930s Stanfords had simply not developed a range of new publications or a presence in the book trade which would secure its position. The Philips take over now freed Stanfords to concentrate on developing another role for itself, namely as a specialist retailer of international maps – the role which Saunders and Stanford had pioneered exactly a century earlier – although the realisation that this was to be Stanford's real future took some time to sink in. By the mid-1950s, a large volume of official mapping stemming from military activities in World War Two was made available to the public – small or medium scale series covering parts of Europe, Africa and Asia. Also surveys were being carried out by European and American agencies in many third-world countries, such as the work of the Directorate of Overseas Surveys, which assumed responsibility for mapping many former British territories in Africa, the Caribbean and the Pacific. Stanfords was a natural choice as a public outlet for many of these maps. Special mention should perhaps be made of the aeronautical chart series O.N.C. and T.P.C. (Operational Navigation Charts at 1:1 million scale, and Tactical Pilotage Charts at 1:500,000 scale) which were developed by the American and British military from the late 1950s, and which were placed on public sale, not only to the aeronautical industry. These charts offered the only available topographic mapping of many regions of Asia, Africa and South America, and formed an invaluable resource which Stanfords sold in huge quantities.

Stanford's staff built up considerable expertise in this kind of material, and they added a further dimension by importing large-scale survey maps from many European countries – France, Switzerland, Italy, Scandinavia, Spain and Portugal. Topographical mapping was also imported from the United States, Canada, South Africa, Australia and many other countries. Geological maps, thematic maps, nautical charts, and historical maps in facsimile were also sourced from around the world. The handling of these map series was time-consuming, specialist work, but it was undoubtedly financially rewarding, and it gave Stanfords a unique reputation as suppliers of maps obtainable nowhere else in England. From the mid-1950s onwards, the aeronautical and military map department was housed in a claustrophobic basement resembling a wartime operations room, an impression reinforced by the grim ex-Sergeant who ran the place. This room survived into the 1980s, as surely one of the oddest and most anachronistic retail units in modern London.

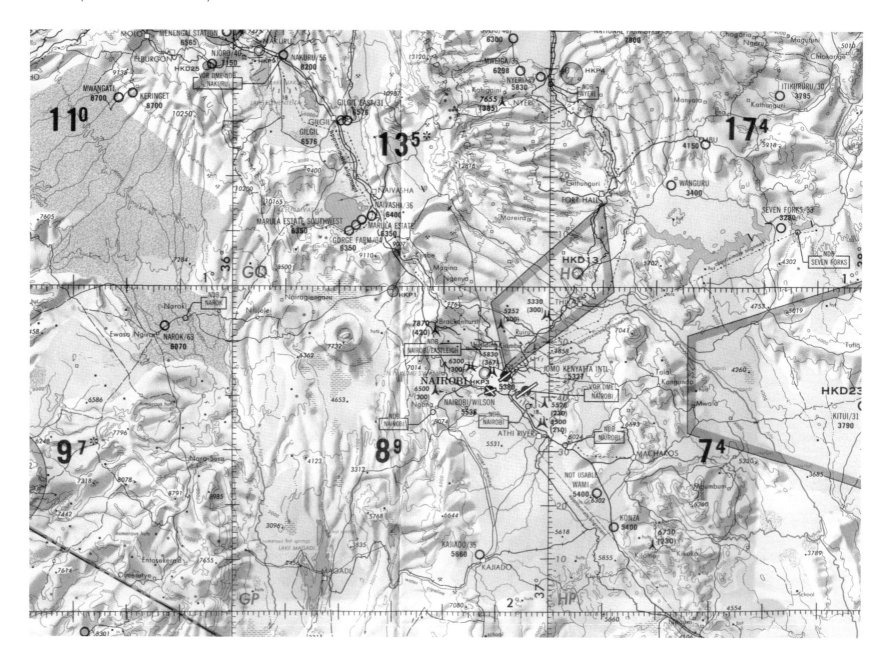

Its closure became inevitable as many of the official map series that originated in World War Two became obsolete, but its passing was regretted by many regular customers; it was the kind of shop department which no modern retailer would dream of creating, and yet it worked impressively.

From this specialist stockholding there grew an outstanding catalogue of national and international mapping, the reference work *International Maps and Atlases in Print* by Kenneth Winch. Winch worked as a map buyer from the late 1950s, and gradually compiled a "Stanford Reference Catalogue" which was held in loose-leaf form, arranged country by country, so that staff and customers could see at a glance the mapping that was available for any region of the world. Its potential as a bibliographical aid was soon realised, and the work was published by Bowker in book form in 1973. For many years "Winch" was an invaluable reference tool for serious map users, and it was the forerunner of later more academic map reference works.

Two events of the 1960s had far-reaching and less positive implications for Stanfords. Firstly in 1962 George Philips' lease on their offices and showroom in Fleet Street expired, and many of the Philips staff were relocated to Long Acre. This made absolutely concrete the realisation that Stanford's independence had gone: since 1946 the new owners had been a somewhat remote power, but now they had taken over the building, and Stanfords was now no more than a name on the door. A few years later came an even more drastic break with the past – the loss of the Ordnance Survey main agency. Relations between Stanfords and the Ordnance Survey had been stormy from the very earliest days. The Survey tended to regard Stanfords as mere salesmen and shopkeepers, while Stanfords felt that the grandees at Southampton were unappreciative of the huge burden which was taken from their shoulders by Stanfords' handling of all public sales. Now in the late 1960s the Survey became dissatisfied with the level of Stanford's sales, while Stanford's parent company was looking hard at the narrow profit margins which they earned for all the immense labour of handling thousands upon thousands of large-scale maps. Persistent problems in monitoring this huge stock of sheets further eroded Stanford's profits. At this time the Ordnance Survey section of the shop was run as a separate entity, where customers and shop staff were forbidden to enter; it was staffed by unionised warehousemen, who were a law unto themselves, and who communicated with the outside world through antiquated message-tubes. This situation could not continue, and in 1969 the Ordnance Survey opened its large new headquarters at Southampton, and they were eager to take back into their own hands the trade distribution of the large-scale maps which Stanfords had handled for so long. After long negotiations the decision was made in 1970, to the relief of both sides: Stanfords' main agency was to end, replaced by an arrangement where Stanford would sell the large-scale maps of a restricted area of south-east England only, while the main agency for sales to the public was transferred to Cook, Hammond and

OPPOSITE: **Detail from an *Operational Navigational Chart of Kenya.* From the 1960s onwards these aeronautical charts published by the U.S. Defense Mapping Agency provided invaluable topographical mapping of much of the world.**

Kell in Westminster; Stanfords would continue to sell all the small-scale maps too. So ended the principal phase of a commercial relationship which had lasted for well over a century. Very soon after this transfer, a major technical innovation saw the large-scale Ordnance plans (1:1250 and 1:2500) printed on demand from microfilm by means of a newly-designed reader-printer. Twenty staff were lost, and the Ordnance Survey department, so long the heart of Stanfords, virtually ceased to exist.

In fact this loss of the Ordnance Survey main agency, combined with the stocking of more and more specialist international mapping, presented Stanfords with an exciting opportunity to strengthen their business identity, for by the 1970s a far-reaching revolution in travel was under way, and Stanfords was uniquely placed to profit from it. The demand for specialist topographical or scientific maps had created a worthwhile specialist service, but serious business growth would come only with the age of mass travel. This revolution had no single origin, but it reflected a number of important changes in British society. First and most obvious was its growing affluence: wealth will always seek new means to display itself, and people began to seek out new travel destinations as lifestyle statements. A holiday in Cornwall or Brittany was timid and bourgeois: Mediterranean islands became the minimum standard of chic; Turkey or North Africa were better; while those really intent on being different were beginning to mention places in East Africa, the Caribbean, or the islands of the Indian Ocean. This search for the exotic would intensify, led at first by the young who took the hippy trail to India and Nepal, but later crossing the social classes, so that expensive trips to the Himalayan kingdoms became commonplace for the middle-aged and middle classes too. The vogue for independent travel or mountain-trekking took thousands of young people to the Andean countries, and the Far East, as well as to the Indian subcontinent, the strong element of political or personal danger in some of these countries adding to the challenge and the achievement. At the same time the price revolution in air fares opened North America and Australia as tourist destinations in a way which they had never been before for English people. The vogue for winter skiing holidays in the Alps also began in Britain in the 1970s.

All these factors meant that the skies over Europe became crowded with unprecedented flocks of people, like migrating birds, caught in a restless urge to criss-cross the globe in search of new destinations. It was the fulfilment of the impulse to escape, prefigured by writers in the 1920s, but now it was world-wide travel for the millions, and not merely for an elite. All this created an outstanding opportunity for a specialist shop selling maps and, increasingly, guidebooks. This opportunity was accentuated by another external factor: in 1973 the Covent Garden Market was closed, and the area became the subject of redevelopment plans which would transform the surroundings of Stanfords into the most exciting shopping district in London. After all the lean years, Stanfords found itself poised on the threshold of a retail boom. Yet there now occurred one of the strangest episodes in the entire history of Stanfords, an episode which brought the company nearer to closure than even two world wars.

Like most London shops the staff of Stanfords tended to be of two kinds: a small group of older employees of very long service, and a large number of younger people, who came and went quickly. By 1978 a group of politically motivated young people had gathered at Stanfords who chose this shop to be the scene of their radical activities. Their primary aim was to create a commune, in which the business was to be transformed into a utopia for its workers. Conventional business principles, such as profit, structured management, or professional goals, were dismissed as oppressive. This group effectively seized power from a weak manager, who somehow persuaded himself that he was taking part in a genuine experiment in workers' democracy. Perhaps it was inevitable that the conduct of this group should, as in all planned utopias, become both arrogant and corrupt. Standards of service in the shop deteriorated, and financial controls dissolved. The specialist nature of Stanford's business was in danger too, as the communards reduced the stock of travel material, and attempted to turn the place into a general bookshop, but with distinctly left-wing, feminist, alternative leanings. For some considerable time the parent company was reluctant to act, but reports of the worsening situation from both customers and from loyal staff became impossible to ignore, and in 1981 a new management was appointed with a brief to bring Stanfords back to sanity. Conflict with the shop floor revolutionaries became inevitable, and in September 1982, on the dismissal of one of them, more than a dozen staff began a protest strike. This was the time when union power was still supreme in Britain, and any strike commanded immediate, blind support from other workers. Stanford's doors were picketed by dozens of people who had no connection with the company, and customers were urged not to enter. Companies with whom Stanford had traded for decades were too frightened to help. All deliveries were cut off. Staff going into work were harassed and threatened, and the police were summoned almost daily to keep the peace. George Philip, the parent company, was terrified that its entire publishing and distribution business would be closed down by sympathetic workers. The crisis lasted for four months, during which time Stanford's losses mounted and the parent company debated whether to close the business. But as so often in the past, Stanford showed an ability to improvise and survive. New staff were recruited – some of them walking in astonishment through jeering picket lines to be interviewed. Goods and supplies were literally smuggled into the building at night. Customers objected to being abused as they entered the shop, but were determined to come back. The strikers began to realise that their aim of closing Stanfords had failed, and after four months they melted away, having acted their brief part in this sorry period in Britain's social history.

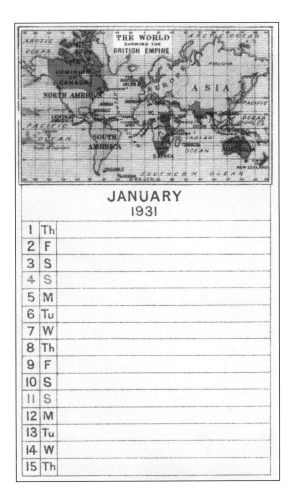

ABOVE: **One of the maps made in 1922 for Queen Mary's famous dolls' house at Windsor, and later reprinted in the pocket-size** *British Empire Diary*; **these were reputedly the smallest maps in the world.**

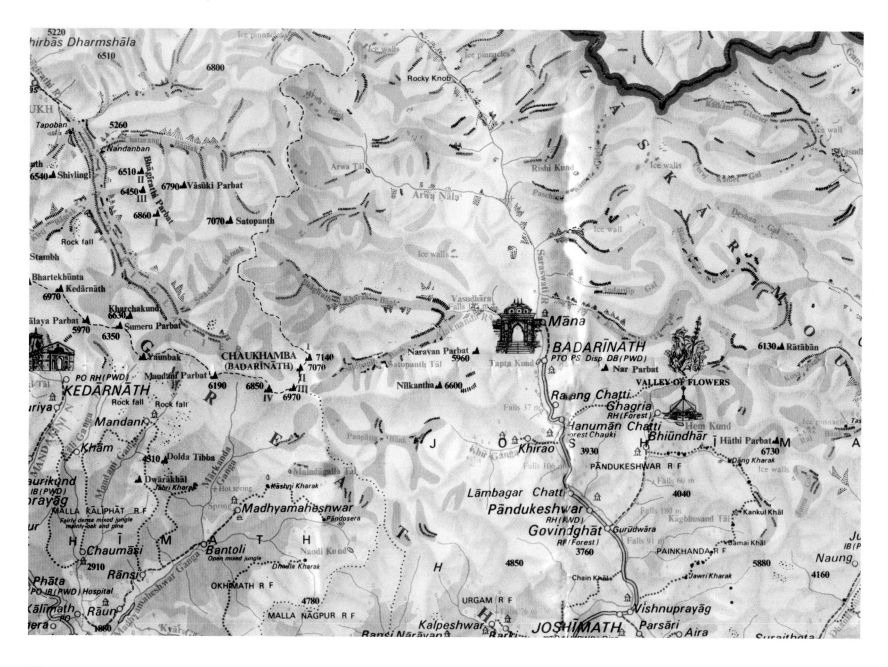

STANFORD CHARACTERS

One aspect of Stanford's story has not so far been discussed in this book – the personalities of the people who have worked there. As always, the generals become famous, while the infantrymen are forgotten. About some one as important as John Bolton we know almost nothing, and there are hundreds of others who are known only as hearsay or legendary stories. There was Mr. Dalmais, caretaker at Long Acre in the Edwardian era, a gloomy teetotaller, who regretted that he could not pour a drink for Mr. Stanford because he had vowed never even to touch a bottle. Mr. Bliss was a senior cartographer after Bolton and Thomas, who used to boast, "Show me any map and I'll guarantee to find a mistake in it." There was Mr. Aistrop, a huge man in charge of the lithographic stones, who could recite in detail all the plots of the novels of Scott, Dumas and Harrison Ainsworth. There was Henry Trevethoe, author of a single wretched novel, who kept a stock of the book under the counter, and when he heard that any customer was leaving on a journey, would sell him a copy to read on the train. There was the persuasive Mr. Morla, who in 1927 convinced the Directors that he could sell large quantities of maps for the company in South America: he was granted £130 in cash for expenses, and furnished with hundreds of map-samples, and . . . was never seen again. There was Bob Glanvil, an impecunious draftsman, always borrowing money from his colleagues, who one day asked a friend for half a crown because he was getting married the next day. There was Morris King, who mysteriously came to work in motorcycle leathers, although he never owned a motor cycle and always travelled by tube. There was Sandra Roberts, the effervescent cashier, a hairdresser by training, who would often help her colleagues by cutting their hair in the postroom during a tea break. After one such session, the company chairman bustled in, and was surprised to notice a large quantity of human hair on the floor; the quick-witted postmaster, Arthur Kiy, suggested that some companies were using it as experimental packing material. It was Arthur Kiy who, hearing of two engagements in one week among the staff, remarked that Stanfords had always been "a very romantic place". There was the elegant and mysterious Amanda Prabhavalkar, with whom at least four members of staff were known to be simultaneously in love. Stanford's staff has included actors and comedians (Kenneth Williams trained there as a map-draftsman), novelists, astrologers, champion cyclists, bibliographers, historians, convicted thieves, and failed poets. All this of course has nothing to do with map-making or map selling, and must await some unofficial historian who can reveal the secret, human history behind that fine architectural façade on Long Acre; but that is another story.

OPPOSITE: **Section of a map of pilgrim routes around Badarinath in the Garhwal Himalayas, published by the Survey of India. This is a typical example of the specialist international mapping imported personally by Stanford's staff.**

123

The seventies had been a wasted decade, but Stanford's moment had now come, and the new management was free to rebuild the company, which they did by training new staff and by setting out to tap the expanding travel market. The shop was enlarged and modernised, and great efforts were made to secure specialist maps from around the world and re-establish Stanford's unique reputation. The Stanford name even appeared once again on some new publications: in 1987 a map of southern Tibet was published, and in 1992 a map of Britain's parliamentary constituencies. Both of these maps were conceived and produced in response to market demands, and curiously, both titles had featured in Stanford's catalogue almost a century earlier. Stanfords was in a unique position to gauge which maps were being requested by the travelling public, but which could not be supplied. It has always taken many years for the main stream map publishers to catch up with changing patterns of travel, and to provide maps of places as diverse as the Gambia, Yemen, the Atlas Mountains, Ecuador or Bhutan.

It is perhaps not widely understood that there are still huge gaps in the available mapping of many parts of the world. The large-scale mapping of many countries in Africa, Asia or South America may be obsolete or unobtainable. Many other countries traditionally regard mapping as a secret or military function, and have refused to place their survey maps on public sale. This was true for many years of the Eastern-Bloc countries, and is still true of Greece and Turkey, many middle eastern countries, India and Pakistan, and China. In some survey authorities, this map paranoia takes the form of an official export ban on maps; in plain language this means that they do not answer letters from abroad, but if you appear at their door, they will sell you their maps. Consequently Stanfords has often sent its own map buyers into Asian and South American survey offices, to stagger out with a year's supply of maps for the shop. Stanfords has prospered in this specialist market because it has taken the trouble to understand changing patterns of travel.

Travel however is not the only source of demand for maps: increasingly it was the news media who turned to Stanfords at times of war or international crises, especially when they exploded suddenly in obscure far-off places. When the Falklands crisis erupted in April 1982, there was a tidal wave of requests for maps of the islands, although the Ministry of Defence moved quickly to ban their sale, lest they should fall into the hands of the Argentinians, while events in the Middle East since the late 1980s have created a huge demand for mapping of that region. During the Cold War years Stanfords was continually visited by representatives of foreign governments – including some pretty shady-looking characters – in search of maps for their political masters. As late as the 1980s, when one would imagine that spy satellite technology was already very advanced, employees of the Russian embassy were buying large quantities of topographic maps for many regions of the world. These "diplomats" used a laughably old-fashioned, cloak-and-dagger

Left: *Map of South-Central Tibet –*
an example of Stanfords recent
return to map publishing, which
concentrates on destinations not
covered by other major map
publishers.

STANFORDS

MAP OF
SOUTH–CENTRAL
TIBET

KATHMANDU – LHASA ROUTE MAP
1:1 MILLION SCALE
ROADS: RELIEF: TRAVEL INFORMATION

BELOW: Stanfords *Map of the Parliamentary Constituencies* was first produced in 1992 and reprints at the time of each general election. It has proved an essential tool for media and public.

approach, grooming the shop staff with bottles of vodka, and paying over large sums in cash. There was little surprise in Stanfords when one long-standing customer – a Russian colonel – was among those finally expelled by the British government for "undiplomatic activities". The map business has always thrived on change – physical and political – and the historic events in Russia and Eastern Europe in 1989–91 created a huge demand for post-Soviet-era mapping, perhaps even more so than the post-colonial era in Africa.

Since the late 1990s Stanfords has moved decisively to reinforce its position in the map and book market. It has opened new shops in Bristol and in Manchester, the first steps towards creating a unique nation-wide group of specialist shops; it has promoted travel literature very strongly by hosting literary events, and by sponsoring lectures by distinguished writers at the Royal Geographical Society; the historic Long Acre shop has been completely renovated and expanded; it has participated in the technological changes at the Ordnance Survey through which the most detailed and flexible mapping is now supplied online; a major investment was made in the company website, which was designed not merely as an advertising platform, but as a complete online catalogue for mail order customers. The seal was set on these changes in the year 2001, when there occurred the most significant event in the company's history for more than half a century: Stanfords de-merged from the George Philip Group, and it once again assumed control over its own destiny. If it is to succeed, any business must somehow mirror the society in which it works. Stanfords grew to prosperity in the 1860s and 70s because it did precisely that, and although its great days of map-publishing are long gone, Stanfords uniqueness still lies in its role as a fountainhead of mapping and travel literature. The history of the company over 150 years has been a microcosm of the history of Britain itself, from the Victorian days of empire to today's era of democratic travel, while its internal achievements and misfortunes have also held up a mirror to British society. In an age of relentless change and uniformity, the map shop on Long Acre remains an outstanding symbol of continuity between past and future.

BELOW: Stanfords *Map of the Parliamentary Constituencies* was first produced in 1992 and reprints at the time of each general election. It has proved an essential tool for media and public.

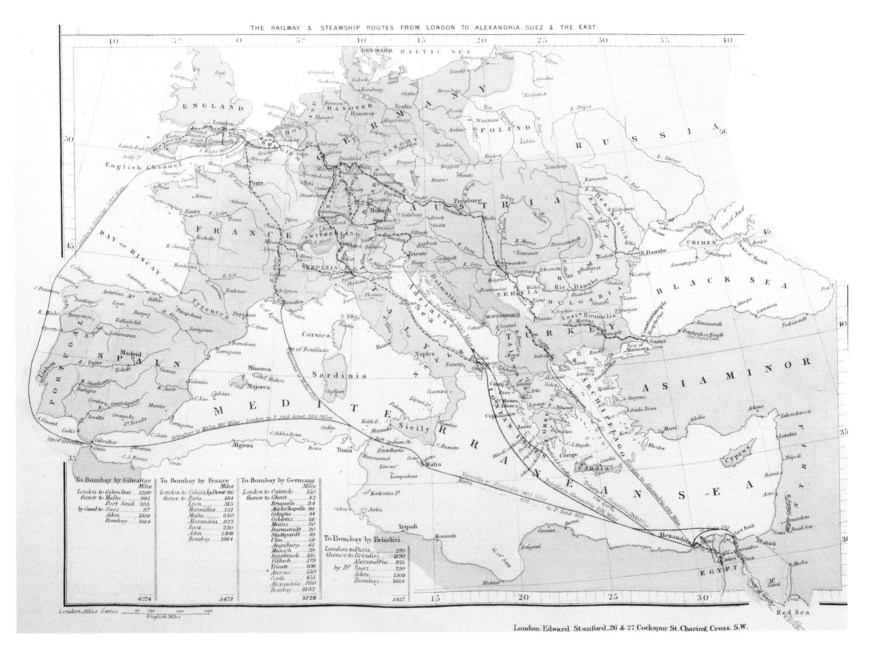

THE RAILWAY & STEAMSHIP ROUTES FROM LONDON TO ALEXANDRIA, SUEZ & THE EAST.

To Bombay by Gibraltar	Miles
London to Gibraltar	1299
thence to Malta	981
Port Said	935
by Canal to Suez	87
Aden	1308
Bombay	1664
	6274

To Bombay by France	Miles
London to Calais by Dover	86
thence to Paris	184
Lyon	315
Marseilles	221
Malta	650
Alexandria	825
Suez	220
Aden	1308
Bombay	1664
	5473

To Bombay by Germany	Miles
London to Ostende	150
thence to Ghent	42
Brussels	34
Aix la Chapelle	96
Cologne	44
Coblenz	56
Mainz	50
Darmstadt	20
Stuttgardt	49
Ulm	58
Augsburg	61
Munich	39
Innsbruck	105
Villach	179
Trieste	106
Ancona	150
Corfu	455
Alexandria	860
Bombay	3192
	5728

To Bombay by Brindisi	Miles
London to Paris	270
thence to Brindisi	1170
Alexandria	825
by Rd Suez	220
Aden	1308
Bombay	1664
	5457

London Atlas Series

English Miles

London: Edward Stanford, 26 & 27, Cockspur St. Charing Cross. S.W.